BRINGING UP JAMIE
How to Raise a Good Kid

Bob Smith (signature)

BRINGING UP JAMIE
How to Raise a Good Kid

Robert C. Miller

 Inkwell Productions

ISBN: 0-974970123

Library of Congress Control Number: 2004102890

Published by
Inkwell Productions
3370 N. Hayden Rd., #123-276
Scottsdale, AZ 85251
Phone (480) 315-9636
Fax (480) 315-9641
Toll Free 888-324-2665
Email: info@inkwellproductions.com
Website: www.inkwellproductions.com

DEDICATION

I don't remember too much of my early childhood of course, but by all accounts I was a noisy, energetic, strong-willed kid, a real load for my mother. I do remember the subject of my childhood behavior being discussed when the family got together, and my parents and relatives laughing and rolling their eyes when they talked about it. And, I remember my dad saying to me during my teens, "One of these days I hope you have a son just like you." I never told him, but as I got old enough to begin thinking about a family of my own, I decided that was the kind of kid I wanted, too.

My son was born in 1970 and I named him after me. He turned out to be exactly what I (and my father) had wished for. Along with my kid, came a lot of unsolicited advice on how to raise him. However, I already knew what I was going to do – I had a game plan.

My son was all of the above, and he tried his mother and me on like so many pairs of new shoes. He would spend all day finding ways we had not already thought of to break or get around our rules. When we told him not to do something, he would look us right in the eye as he did it anyway, waiting to see what our response would be. I absolutely loved it, the idea that this little kid would think that he could get around me; frequently he did of course – I learned as much from him as he did from me. I can honestly say that nothing I have ever done has rewarded me more than raising my kid.

I now have a happy, well-adjusted son who has been a winner in the classroom, in sports and in life. More importantly, he and I are best friends. I dedicate this book to him.

Also, I need to thank my mentor and friend Dr. William

Mundy of Merriam, Kansas, without whose counsel and advice I would not have had the resources to complete this work.

FORWARD

I was born in 1941, just before the United States was drawn into World War II, and grew up in the post-war 1940s and 1950s, a time so remote and different from the present that it is difficult to imagine much less explain. And, I do not refer to the advances in science and technology, although those have been dramatic. No, the changes that amaze me, and probably most of the members of my generation, are the changes in people, in the lives we lead and, most particularly, in what we expect of our children.

My generation was one of optimism and confidence about the future. We walked the streets of our town without fear. Children played unattended in our neighborhoods. When the streetlights came on in the evening we went into our homes, not because there were laws or curfews, but because our parents required it.

Schools were places of learning. We were in our classrooms every day on time with few exceptions. Once there, we accepted the authority of our teachers and confined our raucous behavior to the playground. Those who could not or would not follow rules were disciplined or expelled from school. We were expected to bring home good grades and our parents supervised our homework.

When we accompanied Mom on a shopping trip, we stayed at her side while she went through the grocery or department store. On occasions when we got to go to a restaurant, we were taught to talk quietly and stay in our seats in consideration of other patrons.

At home, we ate breakfast and dinner together at the dining table. We came when we were called and were expected to appear with our hands and faces clean. We were taught to mind our manners and not to make a mess. We stayed at the table until everyone had finished eating.

Our parents chose our clothes and shoes based on what they deemed practical and affordable. Each of us was assigned small duties, or "chores," around the house, which we were expected to do without being unpleasant.

In short, we were taught to behave and to mind our parents.

I do not need to tell you how much things have changed. Children talk disrespectfully and refuse to obey their parents, teachers or anyone else. In shopping malls, stores, and restaurants, parents plead desperately with their disruptive children to behave. Boys and girls yet in grade school run the streets at all hours of the day and night. Old friends invited for a visit bring their children, who monopolize every minute of the visit, and require constant supervision lest they destroy the household furnishings. Classrooms are in a continual state of interruption. Bright children get barely passing grades. Schools maintain metal detectors and locker searches to keep out drugs and weapons. Parents, grandparents, teachers and other adults formerly considered persons in authority are ignored, mocked or even attacked. Children demand and get expensive, brand-name shoes, clothing and other items, for which their parents must sacrifice other family wants and needs.

At the extreme, children commit their lives to drugs, alcohol, cults and gangs, which lead them to lives of hopelessness, crime or both. Teens steal or extort money from family members to support their addictions. High school girls are raped while on a date with a fellow student. Students invade their high schools with guns and bombs directed at their classmates and teachers. Teens spread illegitimate babies, sexually transmitted diseases and violent crime. Teenage suicides increase. Our newspapers and TV's regale us daily with evidence of a society run amok.

These are not the signs of happy, well-adjusted children.

Are these children of today all that different from the children of earlier generations? No, not to begin with. But, they are being raised differently, much differently. And, as a result, we have become a nation of brats, both child and young adult. For whatever reasons, American parents have stopped saying "no" to their children and teaching them to obey.

WHY THIS BOOK?

Walk into any bookstore or library and you can find a whole shelf full of books devoted to the subject of raising children. Articles on the subject appear in newspapers and magazines. Many theories on the subject have been advanced and many methods explained. With all of this information available, why are more and more parents having such a struggle raising their children, and why are they turning out such bad results?

Part of the reason is that life is more complicated now than it was a generation or two ago. But there is more to it than that. I believe that we as a society have gotten away from using time-tested methods of raising our children. Instead, we have pursued one theory after another advanced by experts with impressive degrees and other well-meaning people who have assured us that these "modern" methods will result in our children being happy and well adjusted.

Raising a good kid is time-consuming and will try your patience. But it is not that complicated and, contrary to what you may have heard or read, does not require an education in child psychology. Good people make good parents! If you come into the experience with a willingness to learn and apply a few basic principals, you will have good results – I promise! This book is intended as a simple guide for parents who are beginning the process of raising a child.

APPROACHING PARENTHOOD

I don't want to put added pressure on you as you prepare to enter into this relationship with your child, a relationship that is going to last a lifetime after all. But, what you are about to undertake and how you go about it is very important to you and to your child, and you need to have one thing understood before you begin.

Ordinarily, when you and another person meet for the first time, both of you will find that it takes a little while for you to get to know each other well. That dynamic is also present between parents and their newborn child. However, there is one huge difference. In this case, your newborn does not know who he or she is either.

A child enters the world with no thoughts of who he or she is, what we call self-image or ego. However, children do possess at birth something common to all higher forms of animals, an inborn need to be recognized and accepted by their parent (or parents), together with an instinctive understanding of physical contact, facial expressions, voice tones and body language.

The formation of a child's personality, how he or she acts, thinks and feels, occurs in these early years. Of course the genes you have passed along to your child will play a role in this. But, how you treat your child is going to actually be a key ingredient in the formation of his or her personality. In other words, your child is going to learn about himself or herself from you, the parents. If you look at your child approvingly, speak to your child in gentle tones, stroke your child's skin softly, hold your child close to you, smile when you see his or her face, and even go about the mundane tasks of caring for him or her cheerfully, your child will learn that he or she is lovable and good. If you are frustrated by this new responsibility, find caring for a child to be burdensome, believe that criticism will help your child achieve, have trouble dealing with misbehavior, or frown or speak disapprovingly, your child will come to understand that he or she is the cause of these negative signals and is therefore unlovable and bad.

Millions of people carry with them for a lifetime the psychological burdens of having been raised in a negative environment of criticism and disapproval by their parents. So be sure you bring a positive approach to this experience and maintain that positive attitude at all times. If you do this right it is going to be the most rewarding experience of your life.

THE MAGIC INGREDIENTS

There really is a recipe of magic ingredients, so to speak, necessary for raising a good kid, one who will turn out to be a good teen and a good adult. It is simple, but it is not easy. The two ingredients are love and control. And every child needs both in equal and abundant amounts. Furthermore, these ingredients need to be physical and not merely spoken – they require physical contact between parent and child. Your touch is what your child comes into the world instinctively programmed to need and understand. All higher forms of animals share this need. No amount of talk or adoring looks says love to your child like a hug. And no amount of talk says control to your child like taking him or her by the arm.

I truly believe that your understanding and embracing of this concept is important to your having good results.

SELF-CONTROL AND SELF-ESTEEM

We might disagree about the exact combination of character traits which people need in order to lead happy and productive lives. However, I firmly believe two are absolutely essential: self-control and self-esteem. Furthermore, I believe that these two traits are interdependent, that acquisition of self-control is essential to attainment of self-esteem.

We are a world of many people with differing wants and needs. We are a nation of crowded cities, freeways, work places, schools, shopping and entertainment venues. Moreover, we are a society of laws and regulations, economic constraints, morals and mores, customs and practices. In order to be happy and successful in this life, a person must acquire the ability to control his or her own behavior, to say "no" to himself or herself.

And yet, the signs are all around us that more and more children are being raised in this modern world without ever acquiring the ability to govern their own behavior.

Self-control is not something a child is born with; it is an outgrowth of parental control. It is learned early in life, at the very point where a child begins to think about himself or herself and the people and circumstances that make up his or her world. I am tempted to say "early in life or not at all," but that probably is not completely accurate, although it comes close. Children who do not learn to control their own behavior as a first order of business will find it difficult or impossible to acquire this ability later in life, once personality and behavior patterns have become ingrained.

Whether the child will learn self-control depends on the parents. Self-control begins with parental control, a child learning and developing within a system of reasonable rules and limits established and maintained by loving, positive parents.

The second character trait essential to happiness and success is self-esteem, the capacity to see oneself in a positive way. Although the importance of this character trait begins to show up in the teen years and on into adult life, self-esteem is also acquired in the early years of childhood.

Modern children and teens seem to have everything. Yet the signs are all around us that the young people who are growing up in our time are lacking in self-esteem. Teens turn to hair dyes, unusual and ill-fitting clothing, tattoos, body piercing, and all manner of things to alter their appearance. They seek identity in cults and gangs. They fail to achieve in the classroom. They distance themselves from family. And, in increasing numbers, they take their own lives, having become so hopeless even before reaching the age of twenty that they see no future for themselves.

As a parent, you cannot give your child self-esteem, and you absolutely cannot buy it. Self-esteem is earned through personal accomplishment. It is acquired when a child is raised in a properly structured environment provided by loving and positive parents, learns to control his or her own behavior, learns to make sensible decisions, thus earning his or her privileges and gaining confidence as he or she becomes a responsible person.

I cannot emphasize this enough. No matter what other qualities and talents your child may possess, self-control and self-esteem are essential to happiness and success in the teen years and adult life. A person who does not learn the ability to control his or her own behavior and thus acquires no confidence in himself or herself will always be settling for less.

In this book we will focus on a child from soon after

birth to school age and discuss how you go about loving your child and establishing control, how you remain positive and have fun, and how your child acquires self-control and self-esteem in the process.

MEET JAMIE

Meet Jamie! By reason of substantial literary license, Jamie might be a little boy or a little girl, depending on which page you are reading and the mood of your humble author. Jamie is bright, cute, inquisitive, energetic – all of the qualities you would want in your child. However, lately Jamie is developing another personality trait that is a little more troubling. Jamie is becoming contrary.

The pages that follow are intended to help you understand how children learn to behave as they do, the meaning of this change of behavior, how important this is, and how you should deal with it.

WHY A CHILD MISBEHAVES

Why does a child behave as it does? More to the point, why has Jamie begun to "misbehave"? The short answer is because she has been taught to do so by her parents.

When Jamie was born, she was completely helpless. From feeding her, to changing her wet diaper, to warming her if she was cold, to cooling her if she was warm, Jamie's parents had to satisfy her every need. And, since Jamie came into the world with only one alarm, when she needed something she cried. Her crying set off a search by her parents for the cause of Jamie's discomfort. Was she tired, was she hungry, was she wet, whatever?! If one remedy did not work, the anxious parents tried another until the wailing stopped.

As most would agree, all of this is perfectly normal, unavoidable conduct by parents and their infant child. But, besides satisfaction of Jamie's needs, something else is happening here. As she becomes more aware of herself and those around her, Jamie is learning her first lesson in life: if she cries, her parents (or caregivers) will come to her aid. Jamie is finding out that she is not completely helpless after all, for by crying out she can manipulate the conduct of those around her.

It is the extension and development of this simple concept that sets up the eventual conflict between parent and child, a time known appropriately as the "terrible twos."

THE TERRIBLE TWOS

Jamie's early learning is pretty much a process of adaptation, learning who he is, identifying people around him and learning where he fits into the family routine. But, as his learning progresses he comes to understand that he can exert a degree of control over his environment. As noted above, he has learned that crying brings his parents on the run, seeking to satisfy his needs. As he gains more control over his thinking processes and communication skills, Jamie uses and refines his abilities to manipulate the actions of those around him.

There is no magic starting place for the terrible twos. But, Jamie is a bright child, and well before his second birthday he has a mind of his own and has one thing figured out. He has learned how to manipulate his parents to get what he wants. He knows that if he doesn't get what he wants on first demand, continued howling on his part is likely to spur his parents to greater efforts to satisfy him. Jamie has figured out how to get along in life.

It is important to understand that Jamie does not see himself here as being good or bad. He is doing exactly what he has been taught by his parents, who love him very much, after all. This business of crying until he gets what he wants is what got him this far in life, and he is not about to change now when he is just getting good at it. And, in fact, Jamie is getting quite good at it. By howling for what he wants and refusing simple requests to do things he is asked, Jamie is exercising control over his parents and thus over his own circumstances.

However, and this is *one of the most important lessons* in this book, it is critical that you, as parents, understand what is going on here, and that you set in motion the proper measures to begin correcting Jamie's thinking without delay. For what the terrible twos are about is control. And while Jamie's behavior is the natural result of the way you have raised him to this point, you cannot allow him *at this age* to believe that he is going to make all of his own decisions and to control his own life, and you in the process. You must begin *now* to teach Jamie that you are in charge, and that he must accept your control – in other words, learn to mind his parents. And, you must do this with love and understanding.

As I said above, the terrible twos are about your child learning to accept parental control. It might be helpful here to discuss what the terrible twos are not.

The terrible twos are not about reasoning with your child. There will come a time later in Jamie's development when you will want to reason with her, discuss your thinking about a matter that concerns her, perhaps explain a decision you have made, even ask for her input in arriving at a decision. This is not that time!

Suppose you make a decision, tell Jamie to do something, and she balks. She is not questioning whether your decision is correct intellectually. She is asserting that you are not going to tell her what to do. She is denying your efforts to exercise parental control over her.

How you proceed here is very important. At this age Jamie is capable of absorbing a tremendous amount of information, and is learning from every encounter with you. Virtually every action you take teaches her something about herself, about you and about her circumstances. If you attempt to reason with her about the decision you have made, you have just conceded the most important point in the discussion – that she has the right to question your decision and your reasons for making it. Since control is the real issue here, nothing you say would justify your decision to her anyway. You are not only wasting your breath, you are further ingraining the notion that she is in charge.

Also, there is a hidden danger in reasoning with a child of this age, and that goes to how children learn. If you tell Jamie not to touch a kitchen knife because she might cut herself, and then she touches it and finds it did not hurt her, she has learned a false lesson, one that may result in injury to her later. Jamie does not reason like an adult at this age and is not yet capable of understanding the danger that you see in handling the knife. She has yet to learn how to make decisions and control her own behavior. You must make your decision and make it clear to Jamie exactly what you expect her to do. You must offer no apology or reasoning for your decision. And, most importantly, you must do so lovingly and without anger or disgust.

You might find yourself at this point asking, "What's the big deal about the terrible twos? They only last a couple of years. Why not let them blow over and then let me finish raising my kid?"

The answer is that it is not that simple. The terrible twos represent the only real opportunity you will have in your entire relationship with your child to establish the control you need as a parent to provide for the happiness and well being of that child. Miss this opportunity and another one does not come along. Okay, I am not going to tell you that if you miss this chance you can never make it up. But, the longer you wait the more the odds turn against you. It is a little like setting out to make an earthenware bowl. Begin while the clay is soft and you can make a beautiful bowl. If you let the clay sit until it is nearly dry, perhaps you can still force it into something of the shape of a bowl. But, your end result is going to take a lot more time and effort and will not turn out as good as if you had begun while the clay was fresh.

Your child is now in what are called the "formative years," the time when behavior patterns and personalities are established for a lifetime. However, another time is coming that is as challenging to parents as the terrible twos, and that is puberty, or the teens, when your child begins the transformation from child to young adult. As children enter their teen years, they come to demand more and more freedom from the control of their parents. Teens do need more freedom, but they need to earn it by demonstrating their ability and willingness to exercise self-control and assume responsibility. However, if you have not gained control of your child by this time, you will have no say in this matter. The issue of your powers to exert any control over your teenager will have been decided in his or her mind years ago, and any efforts you may make to impose controls over your son or daughter now will be met with fierce resistance.

These first few years are so critical in terms of the child's development of personality and perception of his or her place in the family. This really is the time to lay the foundation for your child's entire future.

A CLASSIC STRUGGLE

If you read novels or watch movies, perhaps you recognize the elements of the classic struggle here, this conflict between parents and child both seeking to control the terms of their relationship. For, even though this plot will play itself out in your own home for the most part, and all of the parties really do love and need each other, it is going to be a conflict nonetheless. And, I cannot emphasize this enough, it is a conflict that you, the parents, must win. For, it is not only the key to the present relationship between you and your child, it is the beginning of Jamie's learning to accept controls and limits on herself, to make her own decisions, and to assume responsibility, all of which are essential to her future well-being and happiness.

THE IMPORTANCE OF
PARENTAL CONTROL

There are many small reasons apparent on a day-to-day basis why parents need to establish control over their child. There needs to be some routine, some semblance of order in the home, which involves a level of cooperation from all parties, including Jamie. If Jamie is going to balk or ignore you at every turn, refuse to put on clothes, not come to the breakfast table when called, etc., that is going to cause tension, frayed nerves, even flared tempers in the home. As we shall discuss a little later, those are expressions of emotion best left out of the child raising process.

But, there are some big reasons for parental control, too. As much as little Jamie wants to make all of his own decisions, he has not yet learned how to do so. He is not capable of knowing what is good for him and what is not. He does not know how to make sensible choices for his own good. He does not know, for example, to choose foods that are nourishing; he only knows what he likes. Nor does he know all of the risks around him that might endanger his safety, dangers apparent to you but not to a small child.

Suppose Jamie is about to put his hands on a hot stove. There may be no time for discussion, for argument, or for you to intervene physically. There may only be time enough for you to shout a warning, "Jamie, stop!" When such a moment comes, you must have prepared your child to obey you without hesitation or question. The time for Jamie to learn the importance of obeying you, of minding his parents, is not now when the emergency situation is at hand. If Jamie is going to heed your warning in this critical situation you must already have taught him to obey you. And, the same teaching that makes your life with Jamie smoother and happier on a daily basis will also prepare both of you for that dangerous situation you hope will never come, but must be prepared to cope with if it does.

CHILDREN NEED PARENTAL CONTROL

Perhaps you are thinking to yourself that it only makes sense that you are in control of your child. The question is, what does Jamie think? Recently I caught a television show which featured a man who has a large following as a dog trainer. He would take dogs who were discipline problems for their owners – things like running wildly through the house, refusing to stay at the owner's side for a walk on the leash, jumping on furniture or guests, urinating in the house – and would correct their behavior. He was a marvel with the animals, so patient and soft-spoken, and they responded to him. But, most interestingly, he said that when these animals were brought to him, he performed a simple test using body language to determine whether the animal accepted the human being as its master; 85% did not. In other words, almost all of these dogs thought that they, and not their owners, were in control of their relationship. If you can believe that is true for dogs, are you willing to accept the possibility that your bright little boy or girl is capable of these same thoughts?

The fact is that Jamie does not hold any assumption that you or anyone else is in control of her, and her early experiences have given her reasons to believe that she is in charge. This is a lesson that you must now teach her. And, since Jamie does not see any benefits from your telling her what to do, she is going to resist your efforts to control her behavior.

Parental control over children was the norm several generations ago. More recently, perhaps because of changing times or fashionable theories or psychologies, parents have been led toward giving their children more freedom. We have been cautioned against turning our children into "little soldiers," and encouraged to let our children be "free to express them-selves." The advice may have sounded good, but the results have been a disaster.

If you want to see firsthand the products of this unfor-tunate practice, go to a grocery store, a shopping mall or a restaurant where parents have taken their children. You will see and hear children who have been raised to have no respect for their parents – children running wildly with parents calling helplessly after them, children clamoring at the dinner table, parents pleading with their children to behave, even something so ridiculous as a child straining at a harness and leash with his mother at the other end.

Sadly, if you go to hospitals you will also see children who never learned to mind their parents, their bodies burned by fire or hot liquids from the cook stove, mangled by auto-mobiles, broken by falls, or worse, all because the child would not heed a warning from the parent to stop engaging in a dan-gerous behavior before it was too late.

Children do need to develop creativity and do require freedom to function and learn. But the freedom they need is to grow and develop within a framework established by loving parents for their health, happiness and safety. And, as you will see, creating such a framework actually increases the freedom Jamie enjoys to make her own decisions.

NO MEANS NO

The very first lesson in creating and maintaining this framework will be teaching your child the meaning of the word "no." This will come about as Jamie is learning his way around the house and starting to get into everything. But before you can expect Jamie to learn this lesson you as parents must be committed to it. When you say no that has to mean NO! As you will see, this is very important behavior, one that must be ingrained between parent and child.

I mentioned earlier that you never know when you will be confronted with an emergency situation, one where your child's health or safety may be threatened. In the example I used, suppose Jamie is about to put his hand on a hot stove. Or maybe he is about to put some dangerous substance or object in his mouth. There is no time for any other action and certainly no time for discussion. There is time only for the parent to give a warning, "No, Jamie!" When you utter those words, Jamie is only safe if he stops what he is doing without question or hesitation. He must have learned that when you say no you mean it.

All repeated behavior becomes ingrained – it becomes habit. If you sometimes say no and then permit Jamie to continue whatever he was doing, he will not learn to obey you without hesitation. Instead, he will continue doing whatever it was and wait to see what you do next. Most of the time, of course, no harm will come from that behavior. But in an emergency, it may be the difference between Jamie being safe, or perhaps getting a painful burn or swallowing something harmful. The problem is that you never know when you are going to really mean it until you are confronted with the emergency. You must have prepared Jamie to obey you.

So, you need to teach your child that no *always* means no. I believe the one correct way to do this is through physical as well as oral communication. Assume that Jamie has reached for the lamp on a table in the family living area. You would say, "No, Jamie," and then take his hand and pull it away from the object. Most likely he will reach for it again. You repeat, "No, Jamie," and again take his hand and pull it away. You are not loud; your voice is firm but gentle. Do this as often as it takes, and soon Jamie will learn to associate the word "no" with his hand being pulled away from the object. You will detect the first sign that Jamie is "getting it" when he takes his hand away at the sound of your words, even though your hand is not pulling on his. Be sure to praise him when he succeeds.

We will discuss correction of misbehavior a little later in these pages. But for now, it is important to note that you do not correct Jamie here. Rather, you are teaching Jamie correct behavior, teaching him to recognize key words like "no" or "stop," and to associate his behavior with those words. Make sure you don't complicate that process for him by adding a lot of other language, such as explanation. Jamie does not get an explanation of why he is to obey. Otherwise, he will be waiting for the explanation at the wrong time. You want him to associate your words with the need for him to obey. Be prepared to spend some time on this and remain positive. Jamie will learn this lesson quickly enough if you are patient. A negative reaction from you while he is mastering this lesson will only hinder the process.

SETTING LIMITS

All of us, even those who like to think of themselves as free spirits, function within limits of one kind or another – limits imposed by space, time, economic wealth, social custom, religion, employment, family situation, geographic location, health, you name it.

Children are born into a world of limits, at first imposed by their complete dependence upon their parents for the necessities of life. The infants' world is thus limited; they have little or no freedom.

However, as Jamie matured rapidly in the first weeks and months of life, his world began to expand. First he was able to get out of his crib and be on the floor of his home. He learned to crawl and his world enlarged. He learned to walk and his world became still larger. Each step in the maturing process brought new freedom of movement and a larger world in which to move about and explore.

But, as we all know, the larger world contains perils as well as wonders. And, Jamie has no basis of knowledge or life experience to know the difference. What is the difference to a child of 18 months between a sash cord, which may be pulled with little danger, and the electric cord to the coffee maker? Such limits are not apparent to a small child. It is up to you as parents to teach Jamie what limits you are placing upon him and see that he does not exceed them.

In addition to the physical limitations in Jamie's world, there is also the need for behavioral limits. These are a little harder to define and set, and in my experience pose the greatest challenge for the parents of a young child. What we are talking about here is prescribing for Jamie how he must and must not conduct himself in every situation in his young life. And, hardest of all, that he must accept your authority to tell him what he is and is not permitted to do.

We need to distinguish here between setting limits and simply directing your child's activities. By setting limits, I am talking about your establishing boundaries, a structure within which Jamie is reasonably free to operate, to function, to learn and to grow. In such a framework, Jamie is actually making his own decisions and is preparing himself for greater freedom as he matures. He learns where the "fences" are, and knows if he avoids going beyond them, he can make his own choices, for example, what toys to play with, how he entertains himself, and what he does with his time.

In contrast, you must avoid getting in the habit of directing your child's activities completely. If you make all of the decisions about how Jamie occupies his time, he does not make these decisions for himself. Also, this sends the wrong message to Jamie. It tells him that you, the parent, are responsible to keep him occupied and entertained. Lay out fences, and then allow Jamie the freedom to choose his activities. By choosing what he plays with and how he spends his time, Jamie is not only entertaining himself, he is learning to make decisions and how those decisions affect him. And, he is becoming more confident. Play is a very creative process for children. Watch a kid play in a sand pile or with blocks.

Don't get into the habit of setting Jamie's limits solely on the basis of what is easiest for you. For example, it makes less work for you if you set boundaries that keep Jamie and his clothes clean all day, but you wouldn't do that. The important consideration is whether he can learn and grow in the environment you provide. The idea is to set limits that will protect

Jamie while still allowing him the freedom to move around, experiment, and make a few simple decisions. For it is in the making of these first, simple decisions that Jamie learns to be responsible for his own conduct.

Be certain that when you set limits for Jamie, you tell him in plain language what rules you are making, such as confining his play to a certain area. "Jamie, you can play in the yard or in your sand box. But, you are not to play in the street. Do you understand?" Remember, children at this age are still mastering language skills. Little nuances of speech that would be easily understood by an adult are not necessarily clear to Jamie. Also, do not clutter up your instructions with explanations or excuses as to why these limits are being placed; that will only add confusion. Be clear and uncomplicated.

Lack of a clear understanding between you and Jamie about the limits that you are setting for him makes a problem for both of you. Jamie does not know what you expect of him. Frequently, children who are engaging in conduct that might be called misbehavior are, in fact, guilty only of operating in an area where the parents have not set clear guidelines for behavior. If you don't put up the fences, you can't be too upset when Jamie goes beyond the corral.

This is a good time to discuss "loopholes." Frequently when you are laying out instructions for your child you will not think of everything, and you will leave loopholes. Don't worry about trying to find all of these; Jamie will find them for you. After all, this is your kid, so chances are he is just as smart as you. You should never underestimate his intelligence and creativity.

Let's assume that in the example, you come out and find Jamie in the neighbor's yard across the street. You call him and say, "Jamie, I told you not to go in the street." He responds, "No Mommy, you told me not to play in the street. I just went over to play in Randy's yard." When Jamie does wriggle through a gap in your instructions, this is not a time to correct him. He carefully avoided breaking your rule by finding a way around it. Tell Jamie that he is not in trouble, but that you did not mean for him to do that. And that in the future, he is not to go into the street for any reason. Be sure to ask him if he understands and have him acknowledge that he does.

There is another very good reason not to get into the habit of directing your child's activities. Quite frankly, it may be easier to direct Jamie's activities at this early age than to allow him the freedom to make his own decisions. However, soon Jamie will be running and playing in another yard, perhaps at a friend's house, away from your watchful eyes. When he takes those first steps into the outside world where you cannot watch his every move, who will protect him then? The answer is personal responsibility and self-control, which depends upon whether you have done your job of preparing him to accept boundaries you have imposed, and to make decisions within the guidelines you have established. When you tell Jamie he can play in the yard but not to go into the street, he is only safe if you can be sure that he will do as he has been told. If you have not prepared Jamie while he is living in your shadow, he is not going to be ready to accept that responsibility and exercise the necessary self-control when he ventures forth on his own.

PRESCRIBED BEHAVIOR

In addition to setting limits for your child's behavior, you must also set some rules for prescribed behavior. These would include such things as coming to the table when called to eat a meal, coming inside when you call at the door, picking up toys, brushing teeth at bedtime, etc. Most of this prescribed behavior falls within the area of getting Jamie into the household routine. Whether there are just the parents and Jamie, or a larger number of family members, Jamie needs to learn that she is not the only person in the household, and that she has to "fit in." And, she must assume responsibility for doing her part.

For example, when you call her to dinner, is Jamie able to wash her hands and take her seat at the table? If so, then you should not have to walk her through that process each time. Even if it would be simpler for you to wash Jamie's hands and face and seat her at the table, she needs that responsibility and the satisfaction of doing it herself. If you take the responsibility for seeing that those things get done, Jamie learns the wrong thing.

This can be a problem in a household with older children, who may think it is fun to help Jamie. The result is a child who gets used to being "waited on." Obviously, you don't prescribe behavior beyond your child's capabilities. But, once you have determined that Jamie can handle certain responsibilities see that she does. In addition to helping Jamie learn this also cuts down on the number of instructions you give her in a day, a number that can add up and cause tension in the household.

At what age a child is able to do perform certain tasks is related to his or her acquisition of motor skills, the communications between brain and muscle that enable a child to perform certain physical acts. For example, when should you expect Jamie to be able to feed herself, use a spoon, drink from a cup, etc.? I do not claim to be an expert on this topic and suggest that you turn for this advice to the same source I did, your pediatrician, who should be able to help you with this, maybe even recommend a good article or book.

We'll talk more about this later. But the point I want to make here is that you should not set standards for Jamie's conduct that are beyond her physical capabilities. For example, don't take her out of the high chair and seat her at the dinner table until she is able to perform the ordinary functions of feeding herself with eating utensils.

Pushing Jamie beyond her capabilities puts her into situations where she is likely to fail, such as spilling her food on the table. Failure often produces a negative reaction from parents and other family members and sends the wrong message to Jamie, who may be doing her best as it is. Give Jamie tasks she has the motor skills and coordination to learn and praise her efforts, even when she has an accident.

MAKING CHOICES

Your child wants to control his or her own life. However, a child does not come into the world with the knowledge and skills to do so; self-control must be learned from the parents. Jamie learns by making choices of alternatives within his world. In making choices Jamie learns to make decisions. By setting limits and prescribing other behavior, you have taken away some of those choices. Replace those with choices he can make.

It is important that you offer Jamie choices between two positives, and not between a positive and a negative. In other words, don't set up a situation where one of the two choices is to say "no." So you would not ask, "Jamie, do you want to come with me to pick up your dad? If Jamie decides to be contrary and says no, you have a confrontation and a problem. Instead ask, "Jamie, it's time for you and me to go pick up your dad. Do you want to wear your sneakers or your sandals?" You make a clear statement of the context (or framework) and then pose a simple question with positive choices for Jamie to make.

If you think about it, there are lots of small choices that Jamie can make during the day, such as what to wear or what toys to play with. The fact that these choices are trivial to you does not minimize their importance to Jamie. Getting to make these simple decisions gives Jamie the satisfaction of having some personal control of his own life. As he matures, you can put more important matters to him. "Jamie, we are going to eat out this evening before we meet your father, and it is your turn to choose. Where would you like to eat?" Be prepared for burgers and fries, though.

Just as important as your child's personal satisfaction is

what he or she learns in this process. When Jamie makes these simple choices, he is learning to make decisions. As he makes decisions, his confidence grows. Children who have had all of their decisions made for them by their parents become older children and teens who are lost and confused. By asking Jamie to make these simple choices now, you are allowing him to gain confidence and develop his ability to make more important decisions later.

TESTING THE FENCES

So, it is up to you to set some boundaries, a framework within which your child can function. Let's assume that Jamie has decided to play with his ball and you have instructed him that the ball is to stay in the playroom.

Just because you have set limits, do not assume that these are as significant to Jamie as they are to you. Once you have set boundaries for Jamie's play, it is only natural that he should test them. This should not be viewed as an evil or subversive act by your child that should merit your disgust. This is a natural reaction to Jamie finding his activities contained. Frequently, this testing will take the form of an obvious attempt to stretch the fences you have placed.

In the example, soon after play begins the ball comes bounding through the door and into the hall, with Jamie running after to retrieve it, all the time watching for your reaction. If you do not intervene at this point and tell Jamie you expect the ball to stay in his room, he has succeeded in stretching this boundary. Maybe the next time the ball comes through the door it rolls into the next room. Jamie will continue to push and test the rules you have set for him until you insist that they be followed. You are not angry here, just pleasant but firm. "Jamie, if you can't keep the ball in your room, you will have to find something else to play with." Once that particular fence has been made certain, Jamie may go to some other part of the "corral" and start the process all over again. Don't lose your patience. Jamie will be able to sense when he "has you in retreat," and may redouble his efforts to win concessions.

Be certain when you set limits that you are firmly decided about them and communicate them clearly to your child. And, once established, be very careful about allowing Jamie to change them. Once you concede to Jamie that one of the boundaries is not that important to you and can be moved if he wants, the entire corral is in trouble. *Remember, the issue here is not whether these boundaries were perfect, and another set may have been just as good. The issue is which one of you is in control, which one of you is setting these fences.*

Children being raised in such a structure come to expect these limits and rules to be enforced by you, the parents. When they are permitted to ignore boundaries and break rules, they become frustrated and unruly. In other words, even though Jamie tests these boundaries and tries to move them, he really feels more comfortable when you don't go along. He expects you to keep his fences established as they were. When you fail to do your part in keeping his known world intact, he becomes insecure and upset. Jamie is happiest when he is functioning in his world of known limits and expectations.

If you want to observe a good example of this principle, watch what happens when you take your child to anyplace outside the home, such as Grandma's house, church or a restaurant. Little Jamie will begin breaking known rules about as fast as he can think them up. Has Jamie just decided to ruin the evening for everyone? No! Jamie finds himself in a different place and is just testing to make sure that you, the parents, have established his familiar boundaries where he expects to find them. If you do your job and put his fences where they usually are, he soon will conclude his testing and behave normally. However, let him find that you have misplaced one of his familiar fences and he then has to test every one he can think of to see what you have done with all of them.

The lesson here is that if Jamie does not get on the

kitchen cabinets at home, and you want your evening at Grandma's to be pleasant, Jamie should not be allowed to get on Grandma's cabinets either. Even if Grandma wouldn't care, as long as you are there, *you* enforce your rules. When Jamie stays with Grandma, that is another matter.

What about boundaries at Grandma's? Even though most of the time Jamie will be in your home with the familiar limits you set for her, what happens when she goes to Grandma's? The answer is, for the most part, let Grandma worry about that. There certainly is nothing wrong with you giving Grandma some direction about what you expect regarding Jamie's stay, such as her usual bath and bedtime, etc. But you need to realize two things. First of all, Grandma is sure she knows more about raising children than you do, and she is pretty much going to follow her own counsel as soon as you leave. And second, whatever she permits Jamie to do during the visit should have nothing to do with Jamie's conduct once she returns home.

I do not believe in the notion that permissive grand-parents spoil your child's behavior. You should expect that Jamie will find her fences in different locations at Grandma's house – different house, different fence setter. But that does not and must not change the boundaries once she returns home. Oh, you can be sure Jamie will try. "Grandma lets me sit on the cabinets at her house." Your response, "That was at Grandma's. You're home now, and you know you don't get on the cabinets in your house, don't you?" This is not a matter for reason or discussion. And believe me, you are in for a painful lesson if you let Jamie come home from Grandma's and start moving her fences. Remember, move one and all are in doubt.

And, don't think for a minute that Jamie is not smart enough to know the difference. When I was kid, my brother got a dog that he named "Tiger." I remember one time we went to my grandparents' home (about ten minutes from our home) and Tiger went along. We always entered my grandparents' home through the kitchen. This particular time, Tiger stopped as we entered and begged until she got a dish of water; she never got a drink in the kitchen in our house. However, from that day forward, whenever we went to my grandparents' with Tiger, she always stopped in the kitchen and begged until she got a drink. Believe me, Jamie is plenty smart enough to figure out where she is, who is setting her boundaries, and what rules apply in any number of different situations.

Since Grandma has been mentioned, let me interject a word here about the grandparents' role in raising your child. Hopefully you won't have this problem; but some young parents with their first child often find a grandparent intruding into their decision making. You cannot permit this. While it is okay for Grandma to make the rules when Jamie is staying with her, when you are present, Grandma needs to understand that Jamie answers to you. Handle this however you must. But you cannot let Jamie learn that one of her grandparents has the authority to overrule your decisions or that will never end. Make sure Grandma accepts the fact that you are raising Jamie, that you are the final authority where she is concerned, and that you will not have it any other way.

A word about baby sitters. Having a baby sitter come to your house to watch Jamie while you are out for the evening presents a similar situation to taking her to Grandma's or elsewhere. It is the same house, but a different fence tender. You should, of course, give your sitter some guidelines for what you expect. But, you won't think of everything and Jamie will. And, she probably will figure out some way during the course of the evening to commit one or two frauds on the sitter: "Mommy lets me sit on the cabinets when she fixes my dinner (or whatever)."

When you return home, if you find Jamie operating somewhere outside of the fences, you need to remind her, "Jamie, you know better than to be on the cabinets, don't you?" Don't be angry, just be firm. Jamie was only testing to see where her boundaries were set, and when she caught the sitter not knowing where one of them belonged she had to push and test all of them. The real problem here would be if you failed to reset her fences exactly where she expects them to be.

Suppose you are going to take your child someplace completely different than where he or she is accustomed, such as a restaurant for the first time. Don't assume that just because you know how you expect Jamie to act that she automatically knows. Children who find themselves in a new place quite naturally begin looking to see where you have put their fences.

It will make the evening go smoother if you talk about this with your child before you go. Give Jamie some information about the place and what is going to happen, so that she will feel more familiar when she gets there. For example, you could tell Jamie that you will be going in the car to a place to eat called "The Italian Gardens Restaurant," that it will be in a big building with a sign that lights up, that there will be other people there, that all of you will sit together at a table with a red and white checkered table cloth, that they have spaghetti and macaroni (or whatever her favorite foods are), that a nice lady or man will bring everyone's food to the table, and that it is going to be fun. Now, Jamie has some idea of where she is going and what to expect. Looking for the landmarks you have pointed out gives her a reason to be interested. Instead of apprehension of the unknown, Jamie is ready to have a good time with the rest of the family.

A new place means new fence locations, which probably gives Jamie reason to begin testing. So be prepared to spend a little time on this early in the evening making sure Jamie knows what you expect of her. If Jamie does start to stray out of line at the restaurant, don't wait until she is way outside the corral to step in. Just remind her of how you expect her to behave. "Jamie, you don't get down from the table and run around while others are eating, do you?"

HANG IN THERE

This business of setting rules and limits for behavior – telling children what they can and cannot do – is one of the most difficult and yet most important things you must do as a parent. In the beginning, you will get very little cooperation from Jamie, who will resist having her activities contained. Your life experiences have taught you so much that Jamie has yet to learn. You know where dangers lie in ordinary situations, what conduct will be expected of her in the outside world, what foods she must have and what things she should have only in moderation or not at all. Jamie only knows what she likes and that she wants to be her own boss. At this stage of her life it is up to you to establish a framework that will provide for her health, safety and happiness while allowing her to grow and develop, to communicate all of that clearly to her, and to see that she stays within your rules. There is a big payoff at the end of this process, so hang in there!

COMMUNICATING WITH YOUR CHILD

If you think about it, you begin communicating with your child the minute he or she comes into your life. At first, your child only watches and listens, but, within the first year he or she begins talking and gesturing, as well. This is the time to forge communication skills and lines of communication between you and your child that will last a lifetime.

Children come into this phase of development with a personal communication system already in place – they cry or make other noises and point at what they want. Jamie may be reluctant to give up this system, which has gotten him this far after all. So when you see that Jamie is learning words, encourage him to use them. When you are certain he knows how to tell you what he wants and you see him falling back on the old "grunt and point" system, ask him what he wants and encourage him to tell you.

Your child is trying to learn to speak the language by imitating you. So don't fall into the habit of "baby talking" or talking down to Jamie. Baby talk is fine when you are talking to your baby. But don't continue doing it much beyond that point. When Jamie says "wawa" instead of water, it is because he has not yet learned to form all of the vowel and consonant sounds to say the word correctly. However, you don't want him still saying wawa as a four-year-old. So while you would not correct him when he says wawa, do encourage him to learn the language by speaking it correctly to him. Although Jamie may not have mastered adult speech patterns, you should give him credit for understanding more than you think.

The area of communication between parent and child is so important, and unfortunately it is one area where a lot of custom and bad advice have become entrenched in the system. The oft-repeated rules of "children should be seen and not heard" and "children should not talk back to their parents" are not conducive to achieving either your short- or long- term objectives with your child. Setting limits for Jamie's behavior and conducting the day-to-day routine of family life requires good communication both ways. If you adhere to these old rules, you are going to be stifling the growth of Jamie's communication skills.

Rather than teaching Jamie not to "talk back" to his parents, what you should be encouraging is development of good lines of communication between you and Jamie that will last a lifetime. You need to state clearly what you expect. Jamie needs to learn to be a careful listener, to respond to questions and to ask questions of his own if he does not understand what is expected of him. Jamie should be taught to look you in eye and to take his part in any discussion. He should learn to say clearly what is on his mind in an acceptable way

What should not be part of communication between parent and child is harsh voices and hard talk. I wouldn't talk to a dog in the tone of voice I hear some parents use with their children. Remember, this is a child you love. Speak to Jamie in a tone of voice you would use if you were talking with a good friend and teach him to do likewise. You will be surprised at how readily Jamie will accept his role in the communication process and learn to give and take with his parents and other family members.

Children are emotional, especially when they don't get their way. This may bring about situations where Jamie begins "sassing" you, talking in harsh tones or using hateful language. You should not permit this. The rule must be that Jamie can say pretty much what he wants as long as he uses a civil tone and appropriate language. When he does not, remind him that he knows better than to talk like that, and that he should calm down and then you will talk about it again. Allow Jamie to compose himself before you continue the discussion. You are teaching Jamie that there is a right way and a wrong way to communicate. Again, you will be surprised at how quickly Jamie learns to control himself so that he can have his say in matters that affect him.

Remember, it does not hurt to have Jamie disagree with you, even be angry. Those are normal, healthy emotions. The point here is to have Jamie learn to communicate his thoughts and feelings in an acceptable way. If he thinks you were wrong or unfair, and can express that in a civilized manner, he is on his way toward building valuable communication skills for the future.

It is often hard for some parents to accept the fact that their youngster is going to talk back to them. However, there is another good reason for you to consider adopting my method. If you are not willing to listen to all of that childish talk now, it is unlikely that you will have good communications with your child later. Parents who forge good lines of communication with their children as youngsters are able to maintain those lines as their children grow up, and teens really do need to be able to talk to their parents. However, if you wait until then to try to open lines of discussion you probably will find that your child is not interested. So talk with your kid and listen to what he or she has to say. The more you talk with Jamie, the better he will become at listening and communicating his thoughts. And, you will be establishing lines of communication between you that will last a lifetime.

This is a good time to ask the question, "Why do children whine and cry when they don't get their way?" The answer is because their parents have taught them to do so. Children are not stupid. In fact, as I have said before, chances are your child is just as smart as you are. If Jamie whines and cries after the first refusal of some demand and as a result you relent and give him what he wants to "buy some peace and quiet," you are encouraging him to whine and cry the next time he doesn't get what he wants. Jamie is going to use whatever has worked for him in the past. If you sometimes allow Jamie to persuade you when he talks reasonably, but never do when he throws a fit, which method do you suppose he will use?

Your child really is going to learn to talk by imitating you, so you do need to be careful about what you say and how you say it. If you curse, use coarse language or talk ugly about people, your child will learn that from you. So, speak in pleasant tones and say nice things about others, and Jamie will learn to speak in that way too.

One final thought on this subject. Don't forget the importance of facial expressions and body language in communication. Smile and stay positive. Your child is watching you!

LYING AND CHEATING

Development of communication skills brings your child to the point where he or she can relate the details of an incident to you. Unfortunately, refinement of these skills also enables Jamie to add or subtract details in order to explain things differently than the actual events may have occurred. This may happen when a rule has been broken, perhaps some damage done to a household object (like a lamp), and Jamie feels that he may be in trouble. Jamie decides he will lie to you rather then face the consequences for something he did.

You should not permit your child to lie. Lying and cheating, which is a form of lying, are bad habits. Once Jamie finds out that he can lie and cheat his way along in life, avoiding the consequences of his behavior and winning at situations where he otherwise should lose, those will be hard habits to break. So, make it clear to Jamie that you expect him to tell the truth and that you will not accept lying or cheating, and enforce that rule as you would any other for his happiness and well-being.

The difficulty here is that children do fantasize, and you need to distinguish between that and Jamie telling you a lie. Children love "tall tales" and will make up stories about all kinds of situations. I see no harm in that. A healthy imagination is a wonderful gift. However, when you ask, "Jamie, what happened here?" you don't want any stories about space men coming into the room and knocking the lamp off the table. Make clear to Jamie that this is not the place for fantasy or storytelling.

You hope this situation does not happen, but imagine that you find a medicine bottle empty and need to know if your child has swallowed the contents. This may be a situation where, depending on what did happen, you may need to run Jamie to the doctor's office or emergency room. Or it may be something less serious, like he emptied the pills into the toilet so he could use the bottle for something else. When you ask Jamie you need a straight answer, something you can depend on. Teach Jamie the importance of telling the truth and playing fair.

You realize, of course, that if you are trying to teach your child to tell the truth and play fair, you must set a good example. You may still choose to avoid telling Jamie things that you don't want for him to know just now. But, you cannot fabricate facts or falsify information. If Jamie finds out you told him a lie, it is going to be much more difficult for you to ingrain in him the notion that he should be truthful with you.

While we are on this subject, there is a tendency by some adults to cheat in favor of their child, that is to play games and let the child win. This is a situation where a little of that is okay, but a lot is not. I do not advocate letting Jamie win every time you play a game. Life is not going to be like that. By the time he is in school, he is going to have to learn to lose graciously or he won't have any friends. However, Jamie does want and need to win too. Children are not "good losers" and have a short attention span at this age. So, if he seems to be having an unlucky streak, let him win now and then without letting him know that you gave it to him.

VIOLENT BEHAVIOR

Violent behavior cannot be tolerated, and that goes for all family members, or others who may be visiting for that matter. You should never permit your child to engage in violent or destructive behavior or to talk hatefully. I am appalled at the parents I have observed permitting their child to strike them and say things like "I hate you" when the child is denied something he or she wants. Children are emotional, and a child who is denied something he or she wants can be expected to cry; I don't have a problem with that. Crying is a normal expression of emotion, and you should not stifle your child's normal emotions. However, a child should not be allowed to express frustration or anger by striking another person, throwing toys or engaging in other destructive acts.

While we are on the subject of violent behavior, a lot has been written and said lately to the effect that corporal punishment as part of discipline teaches a child to engage in violence. The problem is that corporal punishment while not always violent and harsh can become so. What teaches children to resort to violent behavior is being a party to violent behavior. We will discuss correction later in these pages, and I strongly caution against allowing violence to enter into the correction formula.

Like all other behavior, violence becomes ingrained. Permitting children to express frustration and anger through violent behavior encourages them to continue that behavior through childhood and into adult life. So, children who are successful as children in getting what they want by resorting to violent behavior will continue to do so as they grow into teens and adults. Everyone must learn to live with disappointments and cannot explode into violence whenever they don't get their way. I honestly believe that much of the teen violence we see today is the result of parental failure to curb violent behavior by their children. You should react swiftly and consistently to curb violent behavior by your child. If one of the parents has a problem with violent outbursts, I urge that person to get some help, for your own sake and for the sake of your child.

As a closing thought on this subject, you want to keep in mind here that your child is learning behavior patterns that are going to last a lifetime. If Jamie is permitted to engage in behavior that is violent, belligerent, selfish, inconsiderate, demanding, rude, hateful, disrespectful, etc., or sees you doing so, you can pretty well expect that he will carry those personality traits into his teens and adulthood. No parent wants that. All of which means that you cannot permit such behavior.

CRYING AND TEMPER TANTRUMS

As I have said, children are emotional. You should not suppress your child's normal outlets for his or her emotions. A child who is not permitted to express normal emotions as a child will have difficulty expressing normal emotions as an adult. If Jamie is disappointed or angry about some decision you have made, or something has happened to hurt him or his feelings, it is perfectly normal that he should cry.

While you should not belittle or chastise Jamie for crying, it is perfectly appropriate to try to soothe his feelings, usually with physical contact like sitting on your lap or a hug. The careful reader may have noticed that Jamie is a little boy in this segment. The reason is that parents are more likely with a little boy to say something like, "Big boys don't cry," or some other sage comment to the effect that boys are not supposed to cry. Boys carry into manhood the scars of having been expected to bottle up their emotions as children. All children, boys and girls, need an outlet for their emotions.

However, children can get pretty good at learning to cry "for effect," that is crying to gain attention, which can make things unpleasant for everyone in the household. If Jamie really is venting genuine emotion and not just putting on an act, you should find him receptive to your efforts to soothe his feelings. If he does not want that and continues to wail, he may need to go to another part of the house, such as his room, to compose himself. This is not correction of behavior. You simply ask Jamie to go to his room (or wherever) until he feels like not crying any longer.

While we are discussing this, I need to tell you that the finest "con artists" I ever met were children. Since Jamie has spent his early months of life studying your every gesture, facial expression, body language, voice tone, etc., he has developed the ability to duplicate any or all of them. When you see Jamie appearing to vent his emotions, watch closely. Ordinarily, when Jamie is venting honest emotions, he will be absorbed in himself and will not be paying much attention to you. However, if you observe him constantly looking at you, studying your face, what he is doing is putting on an act and watching for your reaction. What you are seeing is one of his "routines," so to speak. Jamie is trying to manipulate your behavior.

I have used the phrase "manipulating behavior" in these pages, and perhaps that may sound a little sinister. In fact, it is completely normal behavior. All higher forms of animals engage in conduct intended to influence the behavior of those around them. When the family dog puts his paw in your lap and you respond by stroking his ears, he has succeeded in manipulating your behavior. Children become experts at this.

Frequently, if you do not respond to one of these acts, Jamie will try another, hoping to find the one that will change your mind and get him what he wants. Since this is normal behavior, you should not correct Jamie for it. However, you should not have to sit through a long performance of all of his routines either. Children, like all people, need to learn not to "parade their troubles." If Jamie persists, this would be another good time to ask him to go to his room or other part of the house until he is able to gain control of himself.

Anytime your child has gone to his room or other place away from the rest of the family to regain control of his or her emotions, the sooner you can return to a lighter mood the better. If Jamie wants to come back five minutes later and be pleasant, you should consider the preceding events over and done with. You would not bring the disruption back into conversation by going over what just happened. You might ask, "Jamie, are you ready to join the rest of the family again?" If he is, the reception should be positive.

THE NEED TO BE FIRM

There are going to be many times you ask your child to do something or refrain from doing something and are met with resistance. A strong-willed child may be prepared to put up quite a struggle in order to avoid doing something he or she does not want to do, or to continue doing something the parent has ordered stopped. Resistance can take many forms, and Jamie certainly will retain every trick that ever worked in the past for later use. You need to learn to be firm about requiring Jamie's cooperation without "losing your cool." The fact is that you do not need to be unpleasant to stand firmly about a decision you have made, although that is a mistake many parents make.

The old rule about children not talking back crops up again here. Many adults do not like to have some directive they have given questioned by a child, so they become angry or frustrated when that occurs. However, it is completely natural that Jamie should question you. In fact, ask yourself this question: wouldn't you rather have a child with the spirit and the intelligence to ask questions than one who is totally docile and compliant?

You should repeat the directive to Jamie in a calm tone of voice, not showing any disgust or other negative emotion because Jamie has questioned you, and not threatening any correction or consequences. If Jamie still resists, you might simply say, "Come on Jamie, you know what happens when you don't mind your mother (or father)."

I believe there is actually a downside to showing Jamie that he has frustrated you or made you angry, particularly if he is a strong-willed kid. It tells Jamie that his repeated refusals to cooperate have met with some success because he sees you losing control. In other words, if you are able to deal with his failure to cooperate, assert your control and not show any negative emotions, it is a signal to Jamie that you are not about to lose control of yourself and cave in to his demands.

So, remain pleasant, keep your voice calm and hold your ground. I guarantee you one thing: if Jamie manages to make you lose control here, you are the big loser in this exchange and you can count on this happening again.

Since I have cautioned a couple of times already about the importance of keeping the "parental cool," we need to discuss the fact that you will not always do so. Children are keenly observant, so they quickly learn how to "get to you." They become very good at "pulling your strings and pushing your buttons." So what happens when you lose your temper and yell at your kid, or worse, mete out undeservedly harsh punishment for something he or she has done? The answer is you apologize to Jamie just as you would to any other family   member or friend whom you had treated badly. It is important that you do this and do it correctly.

Children have a strong sense of fairness, and Jamie will know if she has been treated too harshly. Tell her that you are sorry that you lost your temper and yelled at her. If you were correcting Jamie for something she did that justified her being corrected, you don't want to lose sight of that in making your peace with Jamie, so be sure that you do not apologize for   correcting her. You should explain that what she did was wrong, but that you did not intend to yell at her (or whatever you did) and are sorry for that. Do not offer an explanation of the reasons why you may have lost control. It is enough for you to apologize for losing your temper. If upon reflection if appears to you that the penalty you meted out was too severe, you should correct that also.

Parents are not infallible, and you should not pretend that you are. Jamie will already know better.

CONSEQUENCES OF BEHAVIOR

Children must learn that there are consequences for their actions. When they behave as they should, they get praise and expanded privileges from their parents. When they misbehave, they are corrected and some of their privileges are withdrawn.

A child who is playing happily within the bounds set by the parents deserves to be recognized and praised. That does not mean that such behavior should be bought. I do not believe children should expect some treat or prize simply for engaging in normal, acceptable behavior. But praise is a great reward for good behavior. And some of that praise needs to be physical. It is great to tell Jamie how nicely he is playing, but nothing creates more positive feelings for a child of this age like a hug or some pats.

In addition to praise from Mom, maybe when Dad comes home from work Mom tells him (where Jamie can hear) how Jamie played today and describes in some detail Jamie's good behavior. This brings a reaction from Dad, such as picking Jamie up and giving him a squeeze while saying how proud Dad is of him. Children at this age thrive on recognition and praise and will make an effort to get it.

Children who accept responsibility and exercise self-control should be rewarded with gradual increases in their personal freedom. As Jamie demonstrates that he is becoming more responsible, he should see an expansion of his privileges and should have more choices about his activities. This will come about as you feel you can trust Jamie more. It is in this way that Jamie's confidence in himself grows.

When you do expand Jamie's privileges or do something special with him because you feel he has earned it, be sure to share your good feelings with him so he can appreciate the rewards of his efforts. I would take my son to some place or event where he was the only kid his age there, and I would whack him playfully and say, "Hey, look at all of the other little kids who are here with their dads." He would look around; then he would grin, whack me back and say, "There aren't any other little kids."

Conversely, all children have "setbacks," times when they have more trouble operating within acceptable boundaries. When Jamie is abusing his privileges and not exercising self-control, he should see a corresponding loss of personal independence. You might even say to him, "Jamie, it looks like you are having trouble playing with your ball today," and remove the ball from the playroom. Jamie will quickly make the connection that when he "plays by the rules" he has more privileges and more autonomy, and will respond by accepting greater responsibility in order to expand his limits.

Parents should never operate on the basis of promises made by their children. "Mommy, I won't do that (whatever it was that you just caught him doing) again! Can I have my ball (or whatever) back now?" Your children earn their privileges and freedoms with their actions. Once you make a decision that Jamie needs to lose some of his personal freedom for a few hours, make your decision stick. That is the only way Jamie learns that he can earn personal freedom or lose it by his actions, that he is responsible for his behavior.

Children, like all people, have their bad days, and there is no doubt that things like being tired or ill affect your child's behavior. However, you want to be very careful about letting these things provide Jamie with an excuse to break rules and exceed limits or be unpleasant. So, do not make excuses for your child by saying things like "Jamie is tired" or "Jamie doesn't feel well." Either of these may, in fact, be true. But saying so sends the wrong message to Jamie. People have to learn to function even when they are having a bad day, and Jamie needs to learn that. The fact that he does not feel well does not justify his being unpleasant to everyone around him or being permitted to engage in prohibited conduct. If you allow that to happen, you will find Jamie having this excuse more frequently.

If Jamie is having trouble staying "in bounds" this afternoon, you certainly don't ignore whatever problem he may have. If he needs a nap or has a cold, take care of that. But, there is a tendency when a child is not feeling well to "let up" a little on the rules for behavior. However, if you permit all of Jamie's fences to be moved because he is ill or tired, you will be contributing to the problem rather that to its solution. Children become more insecure when they find their familiar surroundings have been changed. Believe me, Jamie will be much more comfortable under the circumstances if his known fences remain intact while he is not feeling his best.

REFUSAL TO OBEY

There are going to be times when you get almost no cooperation from your child. Suppose this is one of those times, and now Jamie is refusing to obey you. I am not talking here of merely testing fences. I am talking about Jamie balking or ignoring you when you tell him to do something or stop doing something.

The situation where your child refuses a parental directive or engages in behavior you have forbidden brings you to the point of having to exert your authority over your child. Reams have been written on the subject of how parents should exert control over their children, and all kinds of theories have been advanced regarding whether or not to punish, and what is and is not appropriate. This is my method. It is based on the premise that your child must learn to obey you, and that you can accomplish that in a positive atmosphere. And it works.

It is important to emphasize that you should not become angry at this point. Your voice tone should become serious and businesslike, so that Jamie will know immediately that his refusal is being taken seriously, but not angry or harsh. Also, you want to give Jamie every chance to hear and obey you – kids frequently become "hard of hearing" when they want to ignore you. You should tell Jamie clearly what you expect him to do and that you expect it to be done now. Establish eye contact with him while you are speaking. You should not threaten punishment, but you might ask Jamie if he remembers what happened the last time he didn't mind you. If he now decides that he heard you plainly and is going to do as he was told, that ends the matter. You would not "rub it in" or continue to discuss it. The issue is control, and since Jamie accepted your authority there is nothing more to the incident.

A firmly spoken reminder may be all that is necessary to restore cooperation. But, let's assume that your child is tough, determined and stubborn (like mine was), and that this is one of those situations where Jamie is refusing to behave. You are going to have to correct Jamie's misbehavior.

CORRECTING MISBEHAVIOR

Children are going to misbehave. Jamie really does want to be her own boss and is not going to embrace your rules and directions just because you are her parent. Jamie will operate outside your guidelines and balk or ignore you when you ask her to do something or stop doing something until she becomes convinced that you will not accept her disobedience. All of which means that you must correct misbehavior as it occurs. Stay in control, remain positive, and follow this simple guide.

First, correction should fit the offense. Punishing a child heavily for a minor breach of the rules is not only unnecessary, it is counter-productive. Children develop a sense of fairness early in life, and Jamie will know when you have given her harsher punishment than she deserves and will resent it and you for doing it.

Second, correction must follow the misbehavior as closely as possible. Young children have a very short attention span. Correcting Jamie in the afternoon for something she did in the morning will not deter future misbehavior. She probably won't even remember what she did, and will not understand why you are correcting her.

Third, correction must be consistent. Sometimes correcting for misbehavior which you permit at other times will not deter future misbehavior, because it sends a mixed message to Jamie that correction does not depend so much on what she does as your mood at that moment.

Fourth, correction should be meted out equally by both parents. One parent should not be more lenient than the other or Jamie will detect that. If the two of you have differences about this, work it out among yourselves when Jamie is absent.

Fifth, correction should be handled by the parent who first discovers the offense. If Mom catches Jamie misbehaving, Mom corrects. It is harmful to all concerned to tell Jamie, "Wait until I tell your father what you did." So, when Dad does get home, he does not correct Jamie for the same offense. Once Jamie has been corrected by the parent who witnessed the misbehavior, the incident is over. And even if both parents are present, when misbehavior occurs correction is handled by one; you don't "gang up" on Jamie.

Finally, your choice of what correction to use must be based on results. Over time, the correction you choose *must deter the behavior.* If Jamie does the same thing day after day, you must conclude that whatever you have been doing is not working and that you need to find something else to use as a deterrent. In fact, you are going to find your child willing to accept a higher penalty to engage in some prohibited acts than in others. For example, Jamie may need nothing more than a corrective word to stop splashing water out of the bathtub, but is willing to take whatever correction you have been meting out on a daily basis to go behind the chair and play with the lamp cord. It is your job to find that level of correction your child is unwilling to accept, and then apply it in order to deter that behavior.

That does not mean that you go immediately to the maximum. I like to think about it as "raising the price" a little at a time. If you have ever been to an auction, you know how it works. At the low price, many bidders are willing to pay. As the bidding gets higher, bidders drop out one by one as the price gets too high for them. Correction works in exactly the same way. For some things, Jamie is inclined to drop out at the low price; for others, he is willing to pay more. Your job is to find the lowest price he is unwilling to pay for each offense. It does not require severe punishment to deter misbehavior; it is only necessary that you are consistent in correcting the misbehavior.

In the we have been discussing here, with a positive, loving parent who does not have a problem controlling his or her temper, my preference is for physical correction, that is physical contact of the child by the parent. Being mindful that it is never the purpose of any correction to hurt the child, correction could take the form of a slap on the back of the hand, the snap of a finger against the arm or body, a swat on the bottom, even something so basic as taking the child firmly by the arm. My mother preferred a green switch on the back of my legs – very effective.

Properly used, physical correction has several distinct advantages over other forms of correction.

First, this is the form of correction most readily understood by your child. At this age, Jamie will be more responsive to your touch than anything else. It is your touch that lets her feel and experience your control, and therefore is most effective.

Second, correction is over and done with quickly while the offense is fresh in Jamie's memory. Remember, children at this age have a very short attention span. The most effective correction is that which occurs nearly simultaneously with the misbehavior.

Third, physical correction does not require an extended penalty period during which you cannot return to being more pleasant. Correcting misbehavior is not supposed to upset the entire household.

And fourth, it does not require you to speak in a negative way to your child, which nearly always happens with other forms of correction or punishment that require explanation.

Physical correction meted out in this way by a parent who is fully in control of himself or herself is the best deterrent to future misbehavior – period. Furthermore, physical correction as it is defined here is not violent, and will not ingrain violent behavior in your child.

Correction is never accompanied by harsh language or voice tone. You should never lecture or scold your child. For these purposes, lecturing is a detailed explanation to Jamie of what he did and why he should not have done it; scolding goes the next step and tells Jamie he is bad because of what he did. First of all, Jamie is being corrected for something he knows he should not have done. If he does not know, then you failed to make clear what you expected in the first place, and Jamie should not be corrected for that. A few words to Jamie to the effect that "You know you are not to play with the lamp cord," spoken in a businesslike tone are all the explanation the situation requires. More about this in a minute.

Nor should any warning precede correction. You do not threaten correction. As stated, Jamie knows he is not supposed to play with the lamp cord. He is supposed to leave the cord alone without constant reminders from you. You do not want Jamie to learn that you are going to remind him every time he is exceeding his limits. He has to learn that he is responsible for his own conduct. Unless the conduct is inherently dangerous (such as a hot iron), wait until the offense occurs – Jamie grabs the lamp cord – then proceed to correct the behavior.

Once you have decided that the offense has occurred and made the decision to correct your child, you must do so.

Jamie will stop misbehaving the second he sees you coming. That should not stop you from correcting him. If you stop now, Jamie learns that he can misbehave when you keep your distance, and as long as he stops when you start to come his way he avoids the consequences of his behavior. And, you should not allow Jamie to "plea bargain" his way out of the consequences of his actions: "Mommy, I promise I won't do it again!" You need to realize that Jamie has not made a "religious conversion" here; he is only trying to avoid the consequences of his behavior. He is going to learn something from this experience either way. What you want is for him to learn that he must accept the responsibility for his behavior.

Deprivation is an acceptable form of correction where the offense involves a toy or article that was used in committing the offense or the abuse of some privilege. In the earlier example, this would be the ball that came out of Jamie's playroom. Taking the ball for a few hours is a good way for Jamie to associate his misbehavior with loss of use of his toy and/or loss of privileges. Deprivation should not be used for other offenses. In other words, you would not take the ball away because Jamie refused to stop playing with the lamp cord.

I do not believe deprivation should include loss of normal meals or contact with the rest of the family for long periods of time. Sending Jamie to bed without dinner deprives him of two things he needs for his health and well-being, food and family association. Eating the meal is not a privilege to be taken away.

Grounding, confining your child to his or her room or to the house, can be effective with older children, but not at this age. Small children do not have long attention spans and not only will they forget what they are "in" for, it won't matter to them after awhile. Besides, at this age you want Jamie to think positive thoughts about his room so he can play happily there and go to bed peacefully. That won't happen if you use his room as a detention center.

"Time out" is a form of grounding that recently has become the correction of choice for parents who are trying to gain cooperation from their children. I have several problems with time out. First, since someone has to watch the child to make sure the terms of the time out are observed, it takes your time away from other things you are doing. So you serve a detention right along with your kid. Second, time out takes time during which more positive activities cannot occur. If you were getting ready to leave to go out to eat when the infraction occurred, you either delay your departure by ten minutes, making everyone late, or you elect to let the offense go without correction. Jamie will be able to figure out that angle. Finally, I do not think it is effective in deterring misbehavior, particularly on children of this age whose attention span is not that long. There may be one situation when time out can work for you, and that is to calm a rowdy child who is running and yelling in the house, and needs to regain control of himself or herself. But I think its effectiveness is limited to that kind of situation.

Substitution is often suggested as a means of diverting the child from prohibited activity to something more constructive. An example would be that Jamie is taking knives out of the dishwasher, so you take her and find something else for her to do. I do not like substitution, and my objection goes to what Jamie learns in the process. If you employ substitution on a regular basis, you are teaching her that every time she strays outside her known boundaries, you will take the responsibility of diverting her to something else.

There are two inherent problems here. First, Jamie does not learn that she is responsible for engaging in the prohibited conduct. Second, Jamie does not make the choice of what to do within the environment you have created for her. The goal is for Jamie not to engage in prohibited conduct in the first place, but rather to make her own choices of what she does within the bounds established for her. If you use substitution as your choice of corrective action, be prepared to devote some time to supervision of your child, because this could get to be a game with her. It is okay to help Jamie if she asks you to help her find a toy or something to do, but don't take that responsibility on yourself.

Avoid creating corrections for your child that require bags of your time or upset the entire household. The one who should be paying for Jamie's misbehavior is Jamie, not you and other members of the family.

Another thing to be said for quick correction is that it allows your child to repent from the misbehavior and get everything back to normal quickly. Parents should never hold a grudge for misbehavior or remain unpleasant. This incident is not supposed to upset the entire household for a major part of the day. You are not angry and did not stop loving Jamie just because she broke a few rules. When Jamie is ready to "straighten up and fly right" again, you should be ready to put the incident behind you. If Jamie comes to you for a reassuring hug, so much the better. The return to the lighter, happier mood of the normal routine is as much a part of Jamie's learning process as the corrective action itself. Jamie learns that she is happier when she is behaving within the boundaries you have established. You want Jamie to learn that it is only her conduct that is being corrected. If you continue the unpleasantness long after the offense has ended, Jamie misses that valuable part of the lesson.

We also need to discuss what correction is not.

Correction is not the application of great physical force and painful injury to a child, or causing fear or dread in the mind of a child. Since the term "corporal punishment" has become a loaded phrase in our language, often associated with harsh physical punishment, I did not use that phrase in my book. Parents should never strike a child hard or threaten such action to a child. I have heard stories of fathers who whipped their sons with a belt. You can call that revenge or abuse or even a beating. These actions do not correct misbehavior, and where used will produce only harmful results. Children who have been punished brutally and made fearful by threats of violence carry the scars of that treatment, physical and emotional, through life. A family is no setting for such measures.

Correction is not the means by which you the parent vent your anger at something the child has done or refused to do. In fact, effective correction is rarely meted out by a wrathful parent. When you become angry and lose your temper, what Jamie is going to learn will not be about his behavior but about yours. Whatever misbehavior brought on the episode is lost in the events that occurred after the parent "lost it." Should you find yourself in this dilemma, take a minute to get yourself composed, and then deal with the misbehavior.

Lecturing and scolding are not forms of correction. As we discussed above, you should never lecture or scold your child as part of correcting his or her behavior. Likewise, you should not lecture or scold in lieu of other forms of correction. Jamie already knows what he did; otherwise he would not be getting corrected. And, as you will remember, the matter of why the parent has prohibited this behavior is not open to discussion. At this age, all Jamie needs to know is that you have told him not to do this, and that you expect him to obey you.

Since lecturing and scolding are almost always spoken harshly, I really do believe that they can be psychologically damaging to a child. The stream of criticism delivered in a harsh tone of voice can damage a child's fragile self-esteem and spirit. Jamie was not bad; his behavior was unacceptable. You are only trying to win his conformance to some rules you have made for his happiness and safety. The only words that need accompany your actions here are a simple reminder like, "You know you are not allowed to (fill in the blank), don't you Jamie?"

Never use demeaning words like "bad" or "stupid" or say things like "shut up" to your child. Such words can destroy Jamie's positive image of himself – he comes to believe that he must be bad or stupid or his parents wouldn't say those things. Children carry the emotional damage of such abusive language through life just as they do the scars of physical abuse.

Finally, lecturing and scolding do not deter future misbehavior. Most parents who get into the habit of lecturing and scolding do so to avoid the task of properly correcting misbehavior. Since they are not particularly effective in controlling their child's behavior in this way, they tend to try more criticism and a louder voice instead of switching to something more effective.

Correction is not about humiliating your child in the presence of others. As much as possible, correction of behavior should remain a private matter between parent and child. All human beings, even small children, have a certain human dignity. So rather than correct Jamie openly in front of his playmates or others, call him aside and deal with his misbehavior. If Jamie is misbehaving in a public venue, you might ask, "Jamie, do I have to correct your behavior right here in the restaurant?" Jamie will not want this, and that should be enough to gain his cooperation. However, Jamie needs to learn that you will correct his behavior in public if he leaves you no other choice. Otherwise, he will choose public places for his worst behavior because he feels safe from the consequences.

Correction does not involve contact with the head, face or neck of your child. I cringe whenever I see a parent slap a child's face or box a child on top of the head. It is degrading and humiliating to any individual to be struck about the face or head, not to mention the risk of injury because the child is ducking and moving to avoid contact.

I cannot emphasize this enough. A parent should never punish a child harshly, never give a child a hard spanking and never use harsh tone or hard language in correcting their child. It is only necessary that your child experience your firm physical control in correcting his or her misbehavior. Remember, it is not the severity of punishment that deters misbehavior; it is the consistency of reasonable correction. Not only do force and harsh language not deter misbehavior, the physical and emotional damage that can be done to a child by harsh punishment or language will destroy everything you are trying to do in raising your child.

HOLDING ONTO YOUR GAINS

As you continue to establish your control, your child will be continuing to develop and refine his or her ability to manipulate you in order to regain some of that control. This is completely normal behavior. As I said earlier, your child observes and learns from every encounter and situation. It won't take long before Jamie learns all your personal gestures, voice tones, facial expressions and body language. He will learn what actions set off what responses, and just how far he can push you. In sum, he will become an expert on how to "push your buttons and pull your strings." As I said earlier, some of the finest con artists I ever met were children of this age. Jamie will develop several "routines" of different behaviors designed to persuade you to let him do what he wants. He will be cute, he will be sweet and say please, he will be angry, he will pout. He will say he loves you, and if that doesn't work may he say he is never going to talk to you again. He will shed tears. He may even throw a tantrum. And, he will try any or all of these, one after another, to try to get you to do what he wants.

Since this is about control, you certainly do not want to lose yours here. If any one of these "acts" works to get Jamie his way, you will never hear the end of it. Also, do not get disgusted by this process; this is completely normal. After all, everyone should want a smart, creative kid. And, the smarter and more creative your child is, the more of these routines can be hatched in that fertile mind. Some of the most amusing incidents in my own experience of raising my son were seeing the different acts he put on.

No one is perfect, and you are going to make plenty of mistakes. In fact, sometimes you may feel that you are not doing anything right. However, as we discussed earlier, when you do make a mistake, such as accusing Jamie of misbehavior he did not do, you should apologize. I do not subscribe to the theory of parental infallibility. You know you make mistakes and Jamie does too. If you try to act like you didn't make a mistake, and Jamie knows otherwise, he gets the wrong message. You have just taught him that he is wrong even when he is behaving and following your rules. The better course is for you to apologize for your mistake.

Remember, you should not try to "buy back" your child's good will here. I do not believe in providing treats to make up for parental errors. If you do that, be prepared for Jamie trying to get you into this position again. Jamie just might be willing to take some undeserved correction if it means an ice cream cone later.

Once the incident has occurred and the correction meted out, the event should not be revisited, especially not "thrown up" to the child later as an example of his or her bad behavior. If Jamie commits the exact same violation again, you may want to ask if she remembers what happened the last time she did that. "You got in trouble the last time you (fill in the blank), didn't you Jamie?" But otherwise, I do not see anything constructive in going back over past misbehavior. Your efforts should be toward maintaining a positive, encouraging atmosphere for Jamie. Dwelling on negative incidents from her past behavior is counterproductive.

TRIAL AND ERROR

Learning is all about trial and error – making the choice or attempt and seeing the result. For parents this process translates into extra work.

Little children are not fully coordinated, so they have a lot of accidents. Some of these accidents will result in a mess – juice spilled on the carpet, jelly all over the table, you name it – but be careful not to overreact. Before you conclude that Jamie has broken your rules, consider the possibility that he may have been trying his best and simply "had a wreck." So if Jamie spills something at the dinner table even though he was behaving normally, make sure your reaction is not negative and does not blame Jamie for the effort he was making, such as "Oh Jamie, look at the mess you made." Much better to say something like, "Oh Jamie, don't worry. I know you were trying to be careful," which reinforces the idea of being careful without being critical.

Children also make a lot of mistakes. You cannot possibly tell Jamie everything that he is prohibited from doing, and he will come up with things you cannot imagine. (Recall what I said about loopholes.) Mistakes also make messes – crayon marks on the walls, sand brought into the house, you name it – but again, it is important not to overreact. Remember, Jamie wasn't trying to be a burden to you. Making messes is just part of being a kid. When you do have to clean up a mess, do so amiably and show Jamie how he can avoid having that result next time.

Children love to learn to do things for themselves, things like dressing, tying shoes and brushing teeth. There will be situations every day where Jamie is struggling with one of these tasks, something that would take less time for you to do for him than waiting on him or showing him how to do it. But, don't be too quick to jump in and take over. Let Jamie make his effort and profit from the experience. If you see Jamie becoming frustrated, it is okay for you to say something like, "Jamie, let me know if you need any help with that." But as long as he seems to be working on it, let him see if he can solve it on his own. Jamie will gain a huge boost in confidence when he solves a problem or masters a skill for himself. When he has a "flop," be sure to praise his effort and give him the encouragement to try it again.

On a related subject, some children like to play jokes and surprises on their parents to get a laugh. Some of these are not going to turn out well, but be careful not to throw too much cold water on your child for trying. A good sense of humor is a great aid to get through life, and you don't want to discourage that. So you would not correct Jamie if one of his jokes creates a problem or makes a mess. Perhaps you might smile and say something like, "I don't think that turned out like you wanted it to, did it Jamie? Let's not do that again, okay?"

The fact is that except when he or she is asleep, a child going through the early stages of development is going to require almost constant attention and leave you very little time to yourself. Even when he is trying his best, Jamie will make a lot of extra work for you – needing to eat, wanting a drink, needing to be changed, getting into things, attempting new tasks, making messes, constantly interrupting you, taking you away from other things you wanted to do. And I cannot emphasize this enough. It is vitally important to Jamie that you not show frustration or disgust at his actions. Remember, your reactions to the things Jamie does, your body language, facial expressions and voice tones, give him constant messages of approval or disapproval. An active child will test your physical and emotional reserves every day, and it is so important that you remain positive. Jamie wants and needs to please you. Don't take that away from him by reacting negatively to the extra effort he demands of you. Laugh at his antics and don't be put off by the mess. It is part of having a child.

PERSONALITY TYPES

I want to digress for just a moment to comment on personality types. Just like adults, some kids are placid and laid back, some are aggressive and assertive. You may find yourself asking if these methods take that into account. The answer is yes, these methods work with all kinds of children because the child sets the pace. Keep in mind that your job is not to try and change Jamie's personality or to make her easier to raise. Your job is to help her to grow up and achieve her greatest potential. And don't consider yourself unlucky if your child happens to be one of the aggressive types. What more could you ask than that your kid be smart enough to question everything you tell her, rebellious enough to try every rule you make for her, and assertive enough to look you in the eye and talk to you just the way you talk to her? Yes, she is going to be a little more trying on your patience and energy. But if you do your part, imagine what this child can become.

STAYING IN CONTROL

A final word about this phase of parenting. Do not underestimate the staying power of your child. The more spirited and strong-willed your child is, the longer he or she will be prepared to resist your control. It took my kid more than two years to pass through this stage of his young life, and he was ready to try it again every day. Just stay the course and keep your patience.

I want to offer you an illustration that may help you visualize the task at hand. Have you ever seen a cutting horse work at a rodeo or horse show? If not, the horse with rider, who remains passive in the saddle, goes to "cut," or separate, a calf out of a herd of other calves. The calf wants to stay with his friends, so he tries every way he can to get past that horse and rejoin the herd. But, no matter which way the calf turns, the horse is always in front of him blocking his path. The calf feints and turns and darts from one side to the other, but the horse is always right in front of him. Finally, the calf gives in and allows himself to be controlled by the horse. The horse remains calm throughout the exercise, never showing any sign of aggressive behavior. That, in a nutshell, is your job: always being there, not allowing Jamie to get past you, remaining calm and in control.

LOVING YOUR CHILD

Children thrive on being loved. Just as you can see flowers bloom and the grass turn green after a spring shower, so you can see a child blossom in a loving environment. Moreover, you are in no danger of spoiling Jamie with too much love. I don't believe you can love your child too much.

Expressions of love toward children need to be physical – holding them on your lap, hugging, kissing, stroking, patting, even physical play like rolling and wrestling on the floor. Your touch is what your child comes into the world "programmed" to want and need. Telling Jamie you love him is important. But he needs to feel your physical touch to experience your love in the way that is most meaningful to him.

Perhaps the careful reader has noticed that Jamie is a little boy in this section. There is a good reason for that. Too often it occurs to parents to hug and kiss and stroke their little girl, but not a little boy. Perhaps there is some feeling that little boys are "tougher" and don't need physical affection, at least not from Dad. Nothing could be further from the truth. Children of both sexes need to experience physical love from both parents. If Dad is uncomfortable hugging and kissing his little boy, that is too bad; both would benefit from it. Also, a good romp and roll on the floor, which you know a little boy would like, suits a little girl of this age as well. The hour or so that you get down on the floor to play with Jamie will be the highlight of his day.

You might be wondering here if you can balance these roles of making and enforcing the rules for your child on the one hand, and loving and caressing that same child on the other. In fact, and this is one of *the most important points in the book,* you not only can, you must.

Even it is essential, the setting and enforcing of rules and limits for your child can try everyone's patience. It seems like you are saying "no" all the time, so the process can get a little negative. And, even if they may not intend to do so, parents who are spending a lot of time setting limits and dealing with rules infractions can adopt the appearance of being stern. As discussed above, Jamie is learning from everything that happens around him. If your disapproval and correction of his behavior becomes the only basis for your relationship, it sends the wrong message. Jamie comes to believe that you disapprove of him.

However, in my book, Jamie's parents adore him and understand that his often rebellious behavior is a normal part of growing up. So although they correct his misbehavior, they speak to him in pleasant tones, hold him, read to him, cuddle him, play with him, romp with him, laugh at his antics, care for him cheerfully and express interest in the things he says and does. As a consequence, Jamie loves his parents and wants to please them. Jamie will understand that correction is not of him but is for his misbehavior. Sometimes after he has been corrected, your child may ask, "Do you love me, Daddy?" The answer is, "Yes I do Jamie; that's why I want for you to learn how to behave."

SPOILING A CHILD

I mentioned above some things that will not spoil a child. However, there is one thing that surely will, and that is loving parents who can't say "no" to their child. In trying to show their love and win the favor of their child, they give the child whatever he or she wants and give in to whatever the child asks.

You might find yourself wondering what it could hurt to "light up that little face" by giving your child something he or she wants? After all, at this age, a child's demands are not that much. What harm can it cause?

The harm is that this practice becomes habit. It creates the expectation in the mind of the child that the parents will continue to grant these demands. A child does not have the life experiences to know that this expectation is not reasonable. Furthermore, a child who is being given everything is not earning it, and therefore is not acquiring any confidence in himself or herself. And, since the ugly result of this practice does not surface until it has been going on for awhile, it is an easy trap for parents to fall into.

I am going to switch to another parent and child here because I don't want you and Jamie involved in this episode. Mother and Julie are at the store; Julie sees something, decides she wants it and Mother buys it for her. The next time they go to the store, Julie asks for something else, and she gets that too. At home, Mother cleans up after Julie, picks up her toys, and waits on her. Julie develops cute little ways to avoid having to do things she does not want to do. Her parents lavish adoration on her. And just like my story about Tiger always getting a drink in my grandparents' kitchen, Julie learns how to get whatever she wants given to her.

As this child becomes a little older, the demands increase,

but they are still manageable, so the parents continue to go along. However, something very serious is happening here, something that goes far beyond the monetary cost of buying things or the simple nature of the concessions these parents are making. Giving Julie what she wants is becoming a pattern, and like all repeated behavior becomes ingrained. As her parents fulfill one demand after the other, Julie learns to expect no less. It is an expectation we as adults would immediately recognize as impossible. However, Julie has no prior experiences upon which to base such a conclusion. All she knows is that her parents love her and are giving her what she wants. They buy her things, they wait on her, they let her do whatever she wants. When she gets turned down occasionally, Julie knows how to work on her parents, and they usually give in. The fulfillment of Julie's demands by her parents becomes the basis for their relationship, and getting what she wants becomes a way of life. Julie comes to expect that she will get what she wants because she always has. These parents have set in motion a runaway train.

Little children raised in this way grow into demanding older children, who grow into still more demanding teens. As Julie gets older, her demands are no longer so simple, and often are beyond the parents' means or willingness to provide. The parents want to say no, but there is no easy way to stop. Saying no brings howls of protest from a child who has been taught by these same parents that she is going to get what she wants. The parents, not knowing how they have gotten into this dilemma with their child, give in to some demands and refuse others, always reaping the unpleasant consequences when they deny their child anything. They try to reason with her, only to find her unreasonable. This child has been taught by her devoted parents to expect to get her way, and she is not about to give that up.

As a youngster, Julie cries or throws a fit when she doesn't get what she wants. This is the behavior so familiar to Americans, seeing children wailing at the store or other public place because their parents have refused them something they want or want to do. As she becomes a teen and her demands increase still more, Julie condemns her parents when they fail to give her what she asks, even ridicules them when they plead that they cannot afford it or do not approve of something she wants to do. Some teens whose demands are denied after years of giving in by their parents even become hateful and violent.

I suppose the most common reason for beginning this practice is that it appears to make a little child happy. However, this is a false sense of happiness that soon consumes both parents and child. A child who comes to rely on expectations that cannot be met is not a happy person. Unmet expectations have become a poison to this youngster. She has been taught by her parents that giving in to her demands is a sign of their love for her, and when she doesn't get what she wants, she senses that being withdrawn. The parents are miserable because there is no way now for them to explain why they are denying her that which they so easily gave before. This family is not going to be the happy, loving family it could have been. And this young woman (it could just as easily be a young man), having never learned self-control or attained self-esteem based on personal accomplishment, will go through life facing regular disappointment and failure.

Why have I adopted such a serious tone to make this point? Because the danger is so real and so hard to see when your child is little. As parents, you must learn to say no to your child. You cannot fall into the trap of buying Jamie things or giving into demands to make her happy. Believe me, Jamie will be far happier if you don't ever start down this path. The satisfaction that comes from learning self-control, earning her privileges and assuming her responsibilities will build confidence and self-esteem that will last Jamie a lifetime, and form the basis of a wonderful family relationship, now and for the future. And, Jamie will go out into the world as a teen and later as an adult with the tools to be a productive and happy person.

THE END OF THE TERRIBLE TWOS

I cannot pinpoint the exact beginning of that time in my own child's life known as the terrible twos, which lasted about two years, but I will never forget how they ended.

It had been one of those days when my son had been corrected about umpteen times, and the final time he had gone to his room crying. Usually he didn't stay away long, so when he didn't emerge after about ten minutes, I knocked on the door to his room and let myself in. He was curled up on his bed with his cat. I asked if he was okay. He nodded, but didn't speak. I asked him if he was tired of being in trouble, and he said "yes." I just had a sense that now was the time to talk about this. I said to him that as far as I was concerned, he didn't ever have to be in trouble again, ever, and asked if he would like that. He said "yes," this time in a firmer voice. So, I said this to him. "You know the rules in your house without your mother and I telling you, don't you?" He nodded, so I continued. "When you follow the rules you pretty much get to do whatever you want and you are happy. When you don't, we have to correct you and restrict your activities, and then you are not happy. We don't like doing that any more than you do, but we love you and it is our job. But, if you were willing to take care of your own behavior, then your mother and I wouldn't have to correct you anymore, and you would never have to be in trouble again. Why don't you think about that and let me know."

He came out of his room in about ten more minutes with a big smile on his face, and that was that. Two years of struggle, and in one evening it was over. Oh, we had a setback now and then, but for the most part, after that evening he took care of his own behavior and did not require a lot of correction. From that time on, we were able to go places and do things as a family without much worry about how he might behave. Frequently, before we left the house, I would say to him, "How do you want to do this today – can we just be pals or do I have to spend all day being your father?" He would grin and say, "Let's be pals."

Interestingly enough, I talked to him while I was writing this book and mentioned that evening to him. He remembers it just as I do.

"THAT'S IT FOLKS"

That's it folks, that is pretty much my method, and I hope I made it easy for you to follow. My method is based on physical love and physical control of your child in a totally positive atmosphere. It involves setting guidelines for your child's behavior and expecting him or her to obey. It rewards your child's good behavior with praise and expanded privileges, and corrects misbehavior when it occurs. It allows your child to learn responsibility for his or her actions and to gain control over himself or herself. As your child does those things, he or she will gain confidence and self-esteem and be more capable of the success you hope for in his or her life. Most importantly, your child will be happy and well adjusted, and all of you will have fun being together and doing things as a family, now and for a lifetime.

What kind of results will you have? I believe that if you follow this guide you will have a great kid. Let me tell you what I think you can expect based on my experiences.

By the time my son was age five, we were able to take him anywhere we went, including nice restaurants, sporting events, the theater, wherever. We were not limited to fast food restaurants and other entertainment venues where most parents take their children because they are too rowdy and uncontrollable to take to "nice places." We took vacation trips and our kid would entertain himself en route. He took school seriously, prepared his lessons, and made the grades he was capable of making. We could trust him when he went to a friend's house. He was fun to be with. In fact, he and I spent hours together. Because I didn't have to spend all of my time watching and correcting him, I could take him places he otherwise would not have gotten to go. For example, I love cars, and I could take him with me on Saturday morning to a shop where a friend of mine was working on a car. His mother would take him to the deli and to a movie. The funniest thing though was his attitude about other kids who did not know how to control their behavior. We would be in a restaurant and some kid would be terrorizing the place. My son would grin at us and say, "He doesn't know how to act, does he?"

SOME OTHER OBSERVATIONS

As long as I am writing this book anyway, I want to pass along a few other things I have learned about the process of raising a child that you may find helpful or interesting.

ONE ON ONE

When your first child comes into your life, you will find suddenly that he or she occupies nearly all of your time. Both of you will be involved in everything concerning Jamie and not much else. However, even as you soon realize how important it is for the two of you to keep up your special relationship with each other, it is just as important for Jamie to develop a one-on-one relationship with each of you. This is particularly so if one of the parents stays home with Jamie and the other works away from the home. Maybe the only time Dad spends with Jamie is at home in the evening when both parents are present.

Of course you want to develop a strong family relationship among all of you. But Jamie will develop the closest personal bonds with each parent when just the two of you do something together. I think it is a good idea for each of you to have special activities with Jamie, even something so simple as going out for lunch together. I still remember what a treat it was for me and how grown-up I felt when I got to go somewhere with my dad. So as soon as Jamie becomes reasonably "portable," able to go where you go without too much maintenance, make time for little outings with Jamie, just the two of you. Jamie will come to treasure these times together, as you will.

DEVELOPMENT OF SKILLS

Your child is going to develop rapidly during these formative years, and I want to say a few more words about your appropriate role in this process, particularly what you should and should not be doing while Jamie is growing and acquiring new skills.

All parents want to see their child progress and many love to brag about their child's first words or first steps, but be careful. The role of the parents in this process is to teach, to open the way and give encouragement, not to insist on achievement. You provide a framework within which Jamie can make progress at her own pace. You open doors and push back fences at appropriate times so that her progress is not impeded. You teach and encourage her effort. But be careful about pushing her for greater achievement. It is so important to Jamie to learn to do things for herself – things like dressing herself or tying her own shoes – and she will have to make a lot of attempts for each success she has. Be willing to spend some time with her and, above all, be patient.

I said earlier that children thrive on praise. They also wilt with disapproval and criticism. The self-confidence you are nurturing in your child is very fragile at this age. Even constructive criticism, because it requires an understanding of adult logic and reasoning, is not appropriate for a child of this age. So beware of any expression of disappointment at what you may regard as Jamie's failure to achieve at a particular time. If Jamie is trying as hard as she can to take her first steps, and you show disappointment when she falls, it sends the wrong message. Jamie feels you are disappointed in her. This can be a problem if Jamie is having trouble with something that makes a lot of work for you, such as bedwetting. Remember, bedwetting is not intentional; Jamie does not like this any more than you do. Even children with equal abilities will acquire skills and achieve at different times. So encourage Jamie's efforts, not just her accomplishments. Your encouragement and praise will provide all the incentive and motivation she needs to develop properly.

Even discussion between parents about Jamie's failure to do something that she "should be able to do by now" can damage her self-esteem and her progress. This is particularly likely to occur in homes where the parents have the accomplishments of an older sibling for comparison. Because of the possibility that Jamie or other family members could hear, and the damage this can cause, these conversations should not take place in the home. If Jamie feels she cannot attain at the level of the older sibling, or some other standard that you have set for her, she will satisfy herself with slower progress. Your role should always be positive and supportive, the more so the better.

I am aware of a day-care provider who had marvelous success potty training youngsters by announcing when one of the toddlers in her care went to the potty, which brought applause and cheers from the other kids. Sure changing diapers is unpleasant and is a job you will be glad to be done with. But, acquiring this skill is a big step for Jamie. She deserves praise and encouragement every time she attempts a step in the right direction, and not a negative word when she falls back, as all children do.

FRIENDS

I need to say a few words about your child's early friends here, because of the influence they can have on him or her. Learning to interact and play with other children is such an important step for your child. In fact, if there are no children near Jamie's age in her neighborhood, I believe it is a good idea for Jamie to attend day care a couple of days a week so she can meet and learn to play with other children, rather than spend every day with an adult. And even though they love her very much, grandparents should not provide all of Jamie's care. She needs to learn to socialize with children her age.

The choice of Jamie's friends is important, and you should not engage in any fantasy that your two-year-old has become a good judge of character. Since these are Jamie's formative years, she can learn a lot from the children with whom she has contact, and that could be good or bad. So, before Jamie goes to a friend's house or has a friend over to your house, you need to know about this other kid. Ordinarily, Jamie's early friends live close to home, so you know the family. If this other kid is too disruptive of Jamie's behavior, you need to take that into account in deciding how much time they will spend together.

Also, you should not expect that another child's parents will do everything the same way you do. You need to take that into account in determining how often Jamie will be going to this other child's house.

While we are on this subject, our rule was that children who came to our house to play with our kid followed our rules. For example, you can simply say, "Randy, when you are at our house, we don't throw sand at each other, okay?" When Jamie goes to the neighbor's house to play, she should understand that his or her mother will be watching the kids and setting the rules. For children at this age, I believe the best practice is for you to call the other mom before the two kids get together, just to make sure that you both understand that Jamie will be coming over and that she has the time to watch them.

DAY CARE

Since I have mentioned day care, I want to say a few words about that also. In the ideal situation, you the parents raise your child and you are the dominant influence in his or her life, especially during these early formative years. However, if your circumstances dictate that Jamie will be going to a day-care provider, be aware that this person will be spending a lot of time with Jamie and will also be a big influence in her life. The day-care provider and situation must be chosen very carefully.

Many parents make the decision that both of them will work so that they can provide the "things" their child will need. Actually, Jamie needs you more than she needs these things, so unless it is the necessities of life that this second salary will be buying, resist the urge to go for the money and opt to stay home with Jamie as much as you can. If one of you can work part time so Jamie goes to day care two or three days a week, that is a big improvement over having both parents working full time. As I said earlier, a couple of days a week at day care gives Jamie the opportunity to socialize with other kids her own age, which will be a big help when she goes off to school.

MATERIAL THINGS

Your child is a consumer just like you are. You will be amazed at how quickly your child grasps the concept of having his or her own things. And as parents, this is the "apple of your eye," so you may find it fun buying things for Jamie. We already discussed the danger of buying your child everything he or she asks for. But there is one more thought I want to share with you before you go on your first buying binge. Everyone in the family will be happier if all of you are on the same standard of living.

Parents often feel that they need to sacrifice their own needs so that their child can have "better things." Do not get into this habit. Jamie will not appreciate your sacrifice; he will only assume he is getting what he ought to have and come to expect it. So, rather than gratitude, this practice will only create hard feelings later.

If you are people of modest means, it does not make much sense for you to spend $120.00 for a pair of shoes for Jamie if you are only spending $50.00 on shoes for yourself at a discount store. Jamie needs to learn his place in the family, and part of that is learning to do with what his parents can afford. On the other hand, if you are financially comfortable and regularly buy the best for yourselves, then it only makes sense that you would do the same for your child. So, just as you should not lavish expensive things on Jamie while you scrimp on your own things, you should not spend freely on yourselves while telling Jamie you cannot afford the same for him.

On this same subject, when you buy something for your child, see that he or she learns to take care of it. Don't buy Jamie nice things that he is not mature enough to appreciate and take care of. Having nice things is a privilege to be earned by responsible conduct. If Jamie is old enough to ride a tricycle, he is old enough to put it back into the garage (or wherever you keep it) when he is through playing with it. In fact, one great way to reinforce the idea of personal responsibility is to tell Jamie that he is getting this new tricycle because he has shown you that he is ready for the responsibility of taking care of it, and praise him when he does. If he has a slip up (which he will), such as leaving it in the yard all night, maybe tomorrow the tricycle stays in the garage.

Children are not spoiled because their parents buy them nice things. What spoils children is buying them things just because they see it and want it, or giving them nice things which they are allowed to neglect or abuse. If you will be guided by these thoughts when you buy things for Jamie, you are not in danger of spoiling him.

TOYS

While we are on the subject of material things, this is a good time to discuss toys. Before you begin the process of stocking your child's room with loot, consider this: toys are not merely entertainment for Jamie; play is the way children learn.

Toys are part of the creative and educational process by which a child learns problem solving and decision making, and develops motor skills. Good toys require manipulation and thought in their use. Yet many toys in the stores today are designed only to amuse children. Push a button or pull a string and the toy springs into action. I really believe that the design objective for these kinds of toys is to appeal to children on television. The problem with these devices is that Jamie's role in their use is passive observation, which will occupy very little of his time and from which he will learn next to nothing.

As an example, when I was a kid, my brother got a red fire truck for Christmas. It had cranks to turn, pulleys with string, levers to actuate, and its motive power was provided by my brother pushing it along the floor. He spent hours playing with that truck, building structures out of blocks where there would be imaginary fires, positioning the truck, running the ladder up and down to rescue people. Now, the same truck would have batteries, switches and electric motors providing all the action and would afford no more than five minutes diversion for a child.

So resist the temptation to buy Jamie a lot of entertaining gadgets and get him some toys he can play with.

READING

Recently, I have seen some articles which suggest that reading to your child can be beneficial intellectually. Based on my own experience, I would have to say that is true. I also can say that reading to your child is a wonderful experience for both of you. Jamie is at peace on your lap or next to you on the chair, feeling your touch and hearing your voice. It is among the most positive experiences the two of you can share together. I recommend that you make time for this activity every day if you can. Reading a bedtime story is a good way to get Jamie settled down from more vigorous play and ready for bed. As Jamie grows older, you might get some special books with pictures replacing some of the words so she can read along with you. Children who learn to enjoy reading with their parents at this age can be more readily encouraged to continue reading later, instead of watching television perhaps.

MEALTIME

Children need to learn to feed themselves and can be expected to make a mess when they do. At the beginning, Jamie will need to be fed by her parents. But, when she is able to sit up, she should be given some foods that she can pick up and eat with her hands. You don't want to pick dishes off the floor, so don't use dishes. Just put out a few items on her tray, and let her learn. My kid loved mashed potatoes and would eat them right off the tray with his hands. Children try to put everything in their mouths anyway, so Jamie will catch onto this very quickly. Again, your pediatrician is a good source of advice about what types of foods a child of any age may be given.

There is no doubt that children make a mess when they eat. They are fascinated with the feel, smell and texture of food, and get it all over themselves. So you may feel that it is easier to feed Jamie than put up with the mess. However, the idea is for Jamie to learn that she can feed herself. Plus, children are less resistant to trying different foods in this way than if you try to poke them down.

Mealtime, particularly the evening meal, should be a happy time together for the whole family, and Jamie needs to be included. Try to arrange so that Jamie can eat at the same time and place as the rest of the family. And do not show disgust at the mess – it is part of what you bargained for when you decided to have a kid.

Many children go through a stage where they say no when they are offered a particular food. This could be a genuine matter of taste – it takes time to acquire a taste for certain foods, and Jamie knows what she doesn't like just as you do.

But it could just be Jamie's way of trying to exert some control. When you as a parent give Jamie something to eat, there is an implication that you are telling her to eat it. By saying no, Jamie might succeed in having a choice in the matter, which is important to her. One way to get over this hurdle is to give Jamie the same opportunity to see and choose her foods from the bowl as other family members do. You can hold the serving dishes in front of her and let her make choices. "Jamie, which carrot would you like?

Finicky eating often is the result of children acquiring a sweet tooth before they learn to eat basic foods. Many pre-pared baby foods are loaded with sugar. The advice my pedia-trician gave us was gold: "Don't give him sweets until he learns to eat his other foods."

Also, do not fall into that old trap of staking your repu-tation as a parent on Jamie finishing her green beans, or what-ever. First of all, Jamie may be able to wait you out. And remember what I said about not creating situations where you have to do the penance right along with your child. More importantly, this sends the wrong message to Jamie. Food should not be connected to correction. The idea is to get Jamie to try new things. The rule at my table was that everyone at the table took one serving of every food item to begin with, even if it was only one small bite. If this is something she has had before, you might tell her that the last time she had this she really liked it. Be light and not forceful, so Jamie does not feel that she is being compelled to eat something. If she tries a bite of something and doesn't like it, you should not make a big deal of it. You don't eat foods that you don't like either, and it is not necessary to balance your child's diet at each meal. Give Jamie the opportunity to try this again next time.

Children should not make vulgar sounds or say things like "yuck" at the dinner table to show their distaste for a certain food. If Jamie is to have the freedom to eat at the family table, she must learn an appropriate way to refuse something she doesn't like. Teach her to say something like "no thank you" or "I don't care for any."

I do not believe in permitting children to get up from the table the instant they finish eating so they can resume play. Doing so encourages Jamie to wolf down a few bites and not eat a full meal so she can leave sooner, which means she will be hungry later. If you begin allowing her to leave the table early only to return later and eat, she will insist on doing so every night. The rule at my table was that everyone stayed until the last person was finished eating. As soon as Jamie finds out she is not going anywhere, she will learn to join in the meal, eat until she is satisfied and enjoy the company of the family.

BATHTIME AND BEDTIME

Both bath time and bedtime are going to be regular parts of your child's day, so you want these to be as positive and fun as possible. The routine stays pretty much the same from night to night, so try to work in a few choices Jamie can make and maybe get Jamie some special soaps or bath toys. Perhaps you can have a fun song you sing when Jamie goes to take his bath or to bed. Maybe Jamie wants to be carried to bed or "flown in" like an airplane. The idea is to make the routine fun and interesting for Jamie. You don't want something that gets Jamie too excited, because it will keep him from getting off to sleep. One good idea is to tell Jamie that his bear (or other stuffed toy) is already waiting for him in his bed. Also, this may be a good time for a bedtime story, where Jamie gets to choose the book or story.

Your child's bedroom should be his or her special place. Therefore, this is not a room used for detention. This is a place Jamie likes to go. Do not tell spooky stories in here or talk about what monsters may be under the bed. Also, don't start leaving a light on in your child's bedroom. Children are not afraid of the dark at birth; they only learn that from their parents. Give Jamie as much assurance about his safety and security as he requires. Your assurances should be along the lines that "this is your room and you know it is safe in here."

Your child should sleep in his or her own bed in his or her own bedroom. Letting Jamie sleep with you sounds like fun when Jamie is tiny, but like all repeated behavior it becomes ingrained. It will be difficult to break the habit when he becomes older.

TREATS AND PRESENTS

There is nothing that can get to be a habit any quicker than buying your child something as a treat or present. If you do it once, Jamie will remember that you "always" do. Since treats and presents are so habit forming to children at this age, here are a few thoughts to keep in mind.

Never use treats or presents as a bribe for normal, acceptable behavior. In other words, don't try to buy your child's cooperation with your rules and guidelines. What children get for staying within their guidelines and behaving as they should is hugs and praise. If the two of you are going somewhere together, and you promise Jamie ice cream if she is "a good girl today," she will expect some reward for her behavior every time you go somewhere together. After Jamie has been good all afternoon, there is nothing wrong with telling her that she has been such fun today, and that you are having such a good time that you want to get an ice cream cone. Buy one for yourself too so this becomes a shared moment between parent and child. You have reinforced the idea of good behavior being fun, and Jamie will come to treasure these moments as much as you do, and will not become conditioned that they are a reward for not misbehaving.

Parents often bring presents when one or both of them return from a trip where the child didn't go along. Dad goes to a convention and brings Jamie a present on return. Just remember that if you do this once, Jamie will remember that you always brought him a present when you went on a business trip. So the first time you don't, Jamie is disappointed. I think the much better practice is for Jamie to look forward to seeing Dad because it means resumption of physical contact between them. Jamie gets hugs, maybe gets bounced around on Dad's return. The happiness is felt because Dad is back in the home, not because he brought gifts for everyone. If Dad is going to bring Jamie something, make it simple. Even a few small soaps or bottles of shampoo from Dad's hotel that Jamie can use in his bath will be a treat for him at this age. (I did this with my son, and the first time he went on a trip as a young man he brought back motel soap for me.) Remember, if you bring a lavish gift once, what will you do next time?

Christmas and birthday presents are not given to your child because "Jamie was a good girl." They are given because you love her. That does not mean that you can't engage in the Christmas Santa Claus magic for Jamie. But holding presents for Christmas or any other occasion over a child's head for good behavior sends the wrong message. It tells Jamie that she should expect compensation for following rules and behaving properly.

DUTIES AND CHORES

As soon as your child has demonstrated some acceptance of responsibility and acquisition of necessary skills, you may want to assign him or her some simple duties or chores. This is especially true if other members of the family are pitching in to help around the house. Jamie wants and needs to fit in. However, before you decide you want Jamie working for you, be aware that at this age Jamie will not do any job to your satisfaction

If you decide that you want your child sharing the work around the house, keep in mind that you want for this to be a positive experience for Jamie. At first, give him the simplest task to perform, such as picking up his toys from the floor prior to Dad coming home for dinner. Tell Jamie what you are asking him to do and outline the desired result, and then turn him loose. Let him decide how best to approach the task and do it his way. When he has finished, be sure to praise him for helping. The key is to resist the urge to run right in and straighten up behind him. If you do that, Jamie learns that his efforts didn't count for anything. And if you tell Jamie how he could have done it better, that is going to sound like criticism. If you want the job done differently, the time to make corrections is the next time Jamie is to do this job when you can give more detailed instructions.

NAPS

There is one good reason for a young child to take a nap and that is that he or she needs the rest. If Jamie sleeps through the night and yet still shows signs of tiring during the day, she probably needs a nap. However, neither the nap nor the threat of one should be used to correct behavior. In other words, if Jamie is breaking rules and being difficult, you should not say things like, "Jamie must be tired; Jamie must need a nap." Jamie gets the idea that sleep is a negative thing, something she must do if she doesn't behave. You want going to bed to remain a positive thing. So, if Jamie needs a nap, do not connect it with misbehavior.

SHARING

Children are not naturally good at sharing. While Jamie is learning about "me," she is also learning about "mine!" You can't wait until the first time Jamie is invited over to play with a friend or has a friend over to her house to find out that she will not share toys with her friends. Teach Jamie about sharing while she is little. Whenever you find yourself in a situation where you and Jamie are using something together, perhaps sitting in the same chair or reading the same book, point out to her that what you are doing is sharing. Talk about how sharing is something which two people who like each other can do when they play together. If Jamie learns that sharing is good and fun, it won't be so hard for her the first time she sees one of her friends playing with her things. It is a good idea to give her a reminder before she gets together with her friend: "Jamie, Randy is coming over to play today. You two will have so much fun sharing and playing together, won't you?"

TELEVISION

I have already mentioned television a couple of times, so perhaps you already know how I feel about it. Television has become the "great entertainer" of American children. In some households, the TV set is never turned off. Each kid has a set in his or her room, and everyone watches whatever they want. That was not the rule in my house.

There is a lot of crap on TV, pardon the expression. Even some of the stuff that is rated okay for children has content I did not want my three-year-old viewing. We decided that during these formative years, we would decide what was acceptable for our son to watch. And that, for the most part, he would be better off developing other activities instead of being glued to the TV set all afternoon or evening.

There were children's shows on public television weekday afternoons, and some Saturday morning cartoons that my kid watched. We did not watch the weekday evening sit-coms. In fact, we turned the TV set off at dinner time and did not turn it on again until the ten o'clock news, after my son was in bed. He played with his toys, we played together, we played games, we read.

Television, even good television, has the drawback that it is too passive. Jamie sits there and has entertainment "spoon fed" into his head. He doesn't have to use any motor skills, any imagination or much intelligence to sit and watch TV. Computer games may require a little more interaction, but in my mind they fall into this same category. Even if a little is good, too much is bad. I believe the decline in physical health and increased obesity of American children is related to the fact that so many of them do not engage in enough physical activity, preferring to sit in front of a TV screen or computer monitor. I also think that the sit-coms on TV give a distorted picture of reality and family life, which I did not want my kid to learn at that age. My son would return home on a warm summer afternoon disgusted that he couldn't find any of his friends who wanted to play outdoors – they all wanted to stay inside in the air conditioning and watch TV or play computer games.

TEASING AND KIDDING

Laughing and kidding among family members can be a great way to have fun. Even in a household where everyone loves everyone, there are still compromises to be made every day, so no one gets exactly what he or she wants. Kidding and teasing can release tensions and ease frictions that otherwise might occur. However, little children are sensitive and what self-image they may have is fragile at this age. So, make sure if you tease or kid Jamie that it is light and fun, something she can laugh at right along with you. Never tease a child about something about which he or she is sensitive anyway. Even if you mean no harm, if you see that Jamie is uncomfortable about your teasing her, you need to stop.

FEARS

Children are not born with childhood fears; they learn them from their parents or others around them. If Mom is afraid of bugs and freaks out whenever she sees one in the house, Jamie will be quick to pick up on that. Or if Dad loves to tell stories about monsters or ghosts, Jamie will learn to be afraid of them. Obviously, you want to teach Jamie about things that really are dangerous. But, be aware that if you show your own fears around the house or talk about frightening subjects, Jamie will learn from you to be afraid of those things and carry those fears through life.

COURTESY AND MANNERS

In my generation, children were taught to be courteous, particularly to adults, and to mind their manners. You need only to observe children and teens in any public place to see how far we have gotten away from that tradition. The fact is that courtesy and manners are never out of style. Sure Jamie could get by without much refinement at this age; but he is going to be way ahead later in life if he has good social skills. In fact, nothing will open doors for your child more certainly than common courtesy and good manners. And, the time for Jamie to learn proper behavior is not when he is about to go out the door to his first birthday party at his friend's house. If Jamie is to master these skills for now and for life, you need to make that part of his early teaching.

So, get in the habit of speaking courteously to each other. Say "please" and "thank you" when you ask Jamie to do something and encourage him to do the same. Teach him how to speak correctly when he meets an adult. When Jamie is old enough to sit up at the table and eat with a knife and fork, show him how to sit properly, how to put his napkin in his lap, how to hold his eating utensils. Make it fun for Jamie to learn these skills, and be sure to set a good example. If everyone at home barks at each other, lounges all over the table and shovels food into their mouths with both hands, you can pretty much count on Jamie doing so when he gets invited out.

TRADITIONS

I have spoken of the desirability of building bonds with your child that will last a lifetime. One very good way to do this is to establish some traditions, some things that you always do together. The holidays and birthdays are good times for the observance of traditional practices, but so are other events that occur every year.

Some examples: I have a friend whose dad started taking him hunting when he was a little boy who just went to his 35th opening day with his dad. My wife and I started decorating Christmas cookies with our kid his second Christmas and we are still doing it. Another friend flies to Chicago to go Christmas shopping with her adult daughter, something they have done every year since the daughter was a small child. On my first Christmas Eve, my parents took me to my grandparents' home to celebrate the holiday with them; I went to the family Christmas party in that same home for 50 years, and would not have missed it for anything. My wife's cousin, who has his own business in a large city, still goes back every summer to the farm community where he grew up to be part of the annual wheat harvest. You get the idea. So find some things you can do together with Jamie now and get started making your own traditions. He will come back year after year to share those experiences with you.

MORAL TEACHING

As much as you might prefer that your child always be in the positive environment you have created, you cannot shield him or her completely from "the real world." As Jamie gets a little older and comes into more contact with other people, both personally and through television, it is inevitable that she is going to be exposed to a lot of negative influences. The fact is that hatred, abuse, crime, violence, theft, and many other such things are part of the world we live in. Jamie is going to learn how to deal with these influences from someone – you want that person to be you. Now is your chance to teach her moral values that will last a lifetime.

Here is one situation where the good communication skills you have been building with your child become important. Talk to Jamie about the things she sees and hears. Discuss whether these things are right or wrong. Your explanations and assurances to Jamie that certain things are not right and why they are not, and that the people who do these things should not be doing them, are important to provide Jamie the means to deal with these negative things. Encourage Jamie to ask questions and give her as much information as she wants. Sheltering children from all negative influences is not preparation for life. Real preparation is not only providing the positive influences for Jamie but also teaching her why the negative things she sees and hears are not right and providing her with a meaningful context in which to deal with them.

Also, remember that it is important to set a good example for your child. If you talk ill of others, treat others badly or exhibit poor manners, Jamie is going to have that as her constant example of how to conduct herself.

Finally, this is not a pitch for organized religion. That is a choice each family must make for itself. However, I see a lot of good in Sunday school for kids when they are old enough. The lessons are about loving one another and that is pretty good stuff.

TRAVEL

Sooner or later you will find yourself contemplating a trip away from home, maybe for the holidays or a family vacation, and wondering how difficult it is going to be traveling with your child for the first time. As expected, Jamie will be more trouble than if you had left him with Grandma. But, the fact is that children do not just grow up to be good travelers; they learn from experience. So if you want Jamie to become a good traveler, fun to have on vacations and trips, you need to take him along. A day in the car is a long time to little kid, so start with shorter outings at first and plan some stops where a kid can burn off some energy. And kids are not good sightseers, so don't count on pretty scenery to keep Jamie's interest; take along plenty of things to keep him occupied. But the sooner Jamie becomes accustomed to traveling with the family, the sooner he will learn to enjoy travel and join in the fun.

SIBLINGS

I have alluded to "other family members," so before I conclude we need to discuss what happens should you decide to bring another child into your family. Obviously this will be a big step for you. But, don't forget that this also is going to be a huge change for Jamie. We talked above about Jamie's known world and of the importance of keeping her fences where she expects to find them. When another child is introduced into the home, all of that is going to change. The entire subject material about the roles played by siblings in the family is much too much to be treated adequately in this small book. But here a few things to keep in mind.

If you are family planning, remember that a newborn requires almost constant care. If you introduce this infant into a home where you still do not have the first child under control, you are going to be covered up. It takes most children until around age three and a half to get through their terrible twos and become somewhat manageable. If you are a person who needs some time to yourself, you should take that into account when you are planning the birth of your next child.

Once Mom is expecting, there will be excitement in the family anticipating the arrival of the baby. Jamie wants and needs to be involved in this. So, for example, if Mom has a sonogram done and brings home a picture to show Dad, be sure to share that with Jamie. If Mom can feel the baby kicking, let Jamie experience that moment with her. If Mom and Dad are fixing up the nursery, find some way to involve Jamie. Talk to Jamie about what it will be like when the baby comes and Jamie's important role in this. Give her as much information as possible. The more Jamie feels connected with this process, the less likely she will be to feel left out when the baby comes.

When the baby does arrive, Jamie's known world is going to change dramatically. This probably will cause Jamie to revert to some baby behavior and begin testing fences. All of this is perfectly normal, so stay patient. But recall what I said about making excuses for changing the rules for Jamie's behavior. Jamie will be much happier in this new situation if you keep her fences where she expects to find them. And believe me you are going to get really busy if you have a newborn in the house and let that become a reason to move one or more of Jamie's fences. Remember, move one and all are in doubt.

It goes without saying that you would use this same method in raising the second child (lets call him Junior) as you did in raising Jamie. That does not mean that you should expect the same results. The fact is that no matter how identical you try to make the situation for your second child (or your third for that matter), he or she is not going to turn out the same. Those who have studied in this field talk about the different "roles" played by each child who comes into a family, or the different "paths" each must take. Whatever, the fact is that Junior's situation will not be the same as Jamie's, and he can be expected to develop differently. So if Junior seems to be progressing a little more slowly than Jamie, don't fall into the trap of concluding that he must not be quite as bright. My little brother, who was the second child in our family, managed to barely get by in school and hid his near-genius mentality from our parents until he was 16 years old. As with Jamie, each new child sets the pace for his or her development, with you opening the way and giving encouragement.

Just as important in making the newborn's world safe and secure is keeping Jamie's world comfortable. There is a natural tendency for Mom and Dad to be fascinated with the new baby when he or she first comes home. However, if you allow Junior to occupy all of your attention, no amount of apology or explanation will make Jamie understand and accept this change. When your attentions are withdrawn from her, Jamie will see her brother as having taken her place and be very hurt by this. So be sure to keep as many of Jamie's normal activities as they were – things like playing together, bath time, reading, special outings with one of the parents, etc. And be certain that Jamie gets all of hugs, strokes and reassurances she needs. The idea is for the family circle to expand to accommodate the new baby, not to make room by pushing Jamie aside.

Remember what I said above about some children being aggressive and others being more laid back? You may find that one of your children makes more demands on you than the other. Parents in this situation can find themselves giving that child a lot more attention than the one making fewer demands. However, just because one child demands more of you does not mean that the other child needs less. And don't forget that children are very keen observers. If you slight one child in order to give the other one more attention the slighted child will be quick to pick up on that. See that both of them get equal amounts of hugs, pats and praise.

The introduction of the second child is going to bring a new highlight into your life: sibling rivalry. It is natural that your children should compete for your attentions – all higher forms of animals do this. You may recall how early in life Jamie learned to manipulate your behavior. Well, as soon as this new brother appears in Jamie's house, she will begin learning how to manipulate his behavior. And it won't take Junior long to figure out that he needs to learn how to manipulate everyone if he is going to get what he wants. The result is a household where the kids spend a lot of their time trying to get Mom and Dad's attention and "jerking each other around." This gets to be a game with kids, and it is easy for it to get out of hand.

Just as Jamie learned lots of ways to "push your buttons," each of your children now sets out to become an expert at getting to the other. This manipulation can take many forms – taunting, engaging in behavior to annoy the other, taking a toy that belongs to the other.

One of the most common forms of manipulation is tattling, going to Mom or Dad with information that the other sibling broke some rule or did something forbidden by the parents. You have to be careful how you proceed here. You don't want your kids scrapping all of the time. But if you jump in and correct the apparent "guilty party" you will be assisting one of your kids in the ultimate manipulation of the other – getting him or her in trouble with Mom (or Dad). That is only going to encourage the behavior you are trying to stop. I think the best practice is a twofold approach.

Number one, begin early teaching your children to love each other. Start by including Jamie in holding, hugging and kissing of the baby. Involve Jamie in helping to take care of her new brother by giving her little parts in the routine. When Junior is old enough, get both of the kids down on the floor together for some physical play, where there is a lot of touching and laughing together. Talk to Jamie, and later to Junior, about how they are brother and sister, and about how everyone in the family loves one another, and about how each person in a family helps the other. When they are playing happily together, both kids get frequent hugs and praise.

Secondly, when the behavior manipulation between the

two children gets out of hand, I think the best practice is to separate them for a while, send each one to another part of the house to play. You might say, "It looks like you guys are having trouble playing together, so I am going to separate you until you can be a little nicer to each other." As difficult as it may be to observe, your children really do love and need each other, and will prefer to play together rather than remain   separated. It won't be too long before they are pleading with you to allow them to play together again. Since you are not carrying any grudge here, you would allow this unless and until their taunting gets out of hand, then separate them again, perhaps for a longer period. It won't take very long for them to figure out that you are not going to allow the bickering, and they will learn to play together.

As a final thought on this subject, you should not entertain any notion that Jamie suddenly has become an expert on child care, able to function as a surrogate parent to the new family member. As I said, it is great if Jamie wants to help you with the new baby; the more involvement the better. However, don't give Jamie any encouragement to believe that she is the "boss" over her new brother. It takes a certain level of maturity to be in charge of another person's conduct, and Jamie is not functioning at that level yet. And since you want your kids to play together, you cannot have Jamie trying to govern her brother's conduct – it just creates too many hard feelings and will prevent them from developing a normal sibling relationship. There is nothing wrong with Jamie keeping an eye on her brother, and if he needs something or has a problem she can let you know. But make clear to both of the children that you, the parents, are in charge.

CONCLUSION

Well folks, that really is it! That is just about everything I know on the subject of raising a kid. You probably noticed that there are not a lot of footnotes in this book (as in none). There certainly are more learned tomes out there if that is what you crave. I just do not believe that raising a good kid is a science project, requiring extraordinary training or skill. If you love your child and are willing to apply these few simple principles, you will have good results.

Children are truly wonders. Their creativity and ingenuity will amaze you. They are to be treasured and enjoyed. Many people approach parenthood with the belief that they will not be able to enjoy their child in this way if they spend time correcting behavior. The opposite is true. A child who grows up without parental direction and control is not a happy child. And parenthood is demanding enough without having a family member who is out of control most of the time. Where a child is allowed to dictate the terms of its childhood there will be lack of harmony in the home, frayed nerves, tension, and lost tempers – no one is having any fun. The end result is a kid who never learns to control himself or herself, is not able to make sensible decisions or to assume any responsibility, acquires little self-confidence, will be confused and difficult as a teenager and is unprepared to lead a happy and productive life.

The differences between that child and one raised by the method I have outlined in this book are astonishing. You need look no farther than any public venue to find proof that this is true. Uncontrolled children are crying while their frustrated parents look on with grim faces. By comparison, on the rare occasion that you do see a family in a public place with a well-behaved child, look at how happy they all are and how much fun they are having just being together.

Children who grow up in a positive home and learn from their parents to control their behavior and accept responsibility go on to be happy and productive teens and adults. They become positive and confident about themselves. They achieve at their potential in school, they work hard at their jobs, they are able to make sensible decisions, they have realistic expectations of life, and just as importantly, the bonds created with their parents last a lifetime.

As your child begins life, he or she needs to learn from you that you love him or her very much, that you know what is best, and that you will set the direction for his or her safety and happiness. Love your child and follow this simple guide, and you will have a great kid – I guarantee it!

WHAT NEXT

Your child is five years old. You have followed this guide in raising Jamie, and she is a delightful child. For the most part she minds her parents, she understands about accepting responsibility for her own conduct, she is a confident little kid, ready to enter school. Now what?

The answer to that question can best be given by recalling the process that brought you to this point. Jamie had days when she was on top of her game, when she was responsible and did what was expected of her. Perhaps you found yourselves thinking, "she's finally got it." But then, she had days when she seemed to be going backward, when you thought she hadn't learned a thing. Recall what you did. When Jamie was doing her best, she got praise and expanded privileges. When she was not, you pulled back a bit and took away some of her freedom and perks until she got herself back on track. By this simple process of allowing Jamie more or less autonomy depending on her conduct, you taught her that she was happiest and had the most freedom when she was living within the guidelines you had established for her.

Continue to do this. Jamie will have fewer setbacks now than when she was three, but they will still occur. She will want more and more autonomy. As before, she earns that by assuming more responsibility, controlling her own behavior and being more trustworthy. Jamie establishes the pace at which she is able to do these things; she can have as much or as little freedom as she can handle – it is up to her.

For the next six to eight years, your child's development will be a process of building on what he or she has attained. You will see a lot of personal growth in your child, but the basic relationship you established in these first five years will not change much, except that increasingly you will be able to communicate and solve problems with Jamie on a more adult level. That is all going to change dramatically as Jamie approaches her teens. The onset of puberty is the beginning of nature's process of developing a child's mind and body for adulthood, and it will bring a whole new set of challenges for both you and Jamie. I know you are going to need some new guidelines . . . I'm thinking about it.